Nice My Feelings

Nurturing the Best in Children and Parents

Terry Orlick, PhD

Published by Creative Bound Inc.
P.O. Box 424
Carp, Ontario Canada K0A 1L0
(613) 831-3641

ISBN 0-921165-41-2
Printed and bound in Canada

Book design by Wendelina O'Keefe, Communications Designer

Cataloguing in Publication Data

Orlick, Terry, 1945-

 Nice on My Feelings : nurturing the best in children and parents

2nd ed.
Includes bibliographical references.
ISBN 0-921165-41-2

 1. Parenting.   2. Parent and child.   I. Title.

HQ755.85.074 1995   306.874   C95-900590-0

In memory of my mother
who always knew
how to be
nice on my feelings

Nice on My Feelings

When my child speaks and when she is silent
let me listen to her feelings.
Let me really *listen* and hear what my child tells me.

When she says look at this, let me stop what I am
doing and look now. "In a minute" is eternity, and
the special moment is lost.

Let me remember that her development and sense of value
is more important than anything I am doing.

Let me show my genuine interest in the things that
absorb her and open myself to sharing
those experiences.

Let me encourage her exploration, spontaneity
and creativity.

Let me help her see the good in herself and the
good in others.

Let me give her my most valued possessions:
my time and love.

Let me be nice on her feelings.

Terry Orlick

Contents

Preface

For my entire adult life I have worked and played with children in every conceivable setting. These experiences have enriched me and made me wiser in many ways.

In this book I share with you the wisdom that I have drawn from thousands of children and parents. I offer personal lessons from my own experiences as a parent, teacher, counselor, mental training consultant and researcher in child development. My commitment to children has been guided by my love for the special qualities that live within all children, and all parents—all around the world. These qualities are worthy of nurturing.

Trying to be a good parent is a real challenge for every dedicated mother and father living the complexities of today's world. There are many inherent difficulties that surface as we try to nurture the best in our children and the best in ourselves. I have great admiration for people who excel at parenting and teaching young children, because they are making the most valuable contribution we can make in this world.

If ever we are to live in peace within ourselves and within our world it has to begin with children. It is the only way. If we could implement and live the principles in this book on a global level, there would be no physical or psychological abuse, no need for wars, and all people—young and old—would enjoy higher levels of self-esteem, respect, balance and happiness in living their daily lives. Any steps we can take in this direction are worthy of our efforts.

My offerings are aimed at freeing you and your family to follow a path of love, personal enrichment and excellence in living. Balancing your life is a very big part of this. Somehow you must find a way to respect your own needs as well as your children's needs. This book was written to help you in this quest.

Part I

Respecting Your Personal Needs

Set Yourself Free

Children are reminders of the way we can be
Look closely and you will see
That the essence of childhood sets you free,
Joyful, Spontaneous, Creative,
Playful, Hopeful, Carefree
When the best in you is set free
You radiate warmth, love and intimacy
This essence of childhood lives within you and within me
Set it free, set it free

Keeping the Magic In Your Life

In our early years we are unwittingly coerced into giving up the magic of childhood, and forever after long to gain back the magical qualities we gave up as children.

First, you must take care of your own needs. If you fail to do this, you will fail to meet all other needs as well. When you are feeling best about yourself, you will give your best to others; when you are feeling your worst, you have little or nothing of value to give. This is why it is essential for you to take care of your own needs.

I am not a perfect model of balance but I have worked at keeping a spirit of joy and balance in my day and life. Like most of you, I have multiple demands and responsibilities—to my family and students, to my writing, research, speaking and consulting, and to sharing with parents, teachers, coaches, athletes, children, readers and audiences around the world.

There are times that I feel I spend my whole day or my whole life giving—and getting very little in return. I may listen to 50 or 100 calls, and everybody seems to want something. It's an extremely rare pleasure when someone calls and offers to help me with something, or to give rather than want.

These experiences are reminders that I have to take care of my own needs, as well as others' needs. I have to become responsible for finding a sense of joy and balance in my day and my life. No one is going to do that for me.

Likewise, as a parent you have to find or create situations that allow you to feel positive about yourself and positive with others most of the time. This is your challenge and your responsibility to yourself and your children.

Whenever the demands in your life are increased or excessive, the quality of your life and the quality of your contribution to others is dependent upon finding a sense of balance. Being a responsible parent is clearly a time of increased responsibility and demands. If you fail to meet the physical, psychological and emotional needs of your children, they will definitely be less than their best—maybe for the rest of their lives. If you fail to respect your own basic needs you will definitely be less than your best.

The path to quality parenting and quality living lies in respecting a spirit of balance within the different loves in your life. For me balance is finding beauty, passion and meaning in different parts of my life and living those passions. Balance is learning to really live your loves—at home, at work, in relationships, in nature, music or sport. Balance is respecting your needs for attachment and detachment, work and play, activity and relaxation, giving and receiving, time for others and time for yourself, teaching and learning, intimacy and personal space.

Balance does not mean that you spend equal time with the different loves of your life. It is not a question of equal time, but rather what you do with your time and focus in different domains, for example at work, at home or away from home. Balance is a question of carrying a spirit of joy and connection into the various experiences, relationships or domains that you live.

The path to balanced excellence lies in:
- Being all here when you are here.
- Shifting positive focus from one domain, person or experience to the next—so you can "be" wherever you are totally.
- Respecting your basic needs for activity, rest, nutrition, intimacy and personal space.
- Living magic moments—alone, with others and in nature.

Living Magic Moments

Life is a series of ups and downs for all of us, but ultimately life is what you dwell on. Life is what you focus on. If you dwell on the negative, life is negative. If you dwell on magic moments, life is positive.

The problem with focusing on the negative is that you drag yourself down, you drag others down and you teach your children to dwell on the negative side of life. The advantage of focusing on magic moments is that you lift your life, with your children, friends and loved ones, with your physical pursuits, nature and personal growth.

Ordinary things give birth to an abundance of magic moments. The magic lies in discovering the extra in the ordinary, in finding your way deeper into daily experiences that can lift your day (and your life). Don't live life on the surface. Dive into the experience. Joy lives in the depth and magic of simple experiences, in the intimacy and connection within relationships, nature, feelings, solitude, silence and personal growth.

There are magic moments in almost everything you do. Whether you go for a walk, run, talk with someone, work on a project or play with a child, there are moments that are particularly absorbing, special or magical. These moments may only last a short time but they are pure magic.

When you open your arms and heart to these moments, when you are receptive to them, acknowledge them, accept them, and soak in them, you enrich your life immensely. There is magic in living these moments, in sharing them with others and in reliving them in your mind at the end of your day. Thinking of a magic moment from the past or anticipating one in the future can itself create a magic feeling.

Magic feelings are easier to experience when you carry a perspective of childhood, innocence and openness into your pursuits, as if you are roaming through the woods or through your day playfully, connecting fully with one experience after another. Balance lives in nurturing this perspective in our children and rekindling it within ourselves. If you remind yourself to look for the magic moments *before* you set out to do something, you will almost always find some magic, even in situations you may not normally enjoy.

Questions for You

What are your magic moments?

What kinds of experiences really lift your day and your life?

What are the things that give you the most pleasure or joy?

What are your real loves?

Do you dwell on the negative things in life or on magic moments?

Do you open yourself to really experience magic moments during your day?

How many magic moments did you allow yourself to experience today?

Think about it. If you can open this door within yourself and your children it will make a huge difference with respect to balance and joy in life.

Magic Zones

Magic moments are readily available to you in the following six life zones: Human Contact, Physical Activity, Nature, Personal Accomplishments, Sensual Pleasures and Uplifting Diversion.

Human contact encompasses positive physical, mental, emotional, verbal or social interaction with your children, partner, family members, friends, acquaintances, special people or pets. The magic often comes from a sense of love and acceptance generated within these experiences.

Physical activity, play or sport includes joyful physical activity, exercise, play, games or sport. The magic comes from being absorbed in the activity itself, from positive interaction with others or from a sense of personal achievement.

Nature offers numerous opportunities for positive physical, emotional or spiritual connection within a natural environment. The magic comes from experiencing the beauty, inspiration, excitement, tranquility and wonder of nature itself, and from experiencing nature together with family, friends and loved ones.

Personal accomplishments consist of positive feelings generated through achieving goals, finishing tasks, doing something well, making a meaningful contribution, learning, creating and discovering, and experiencing insights or personal growth. The magic comes from feeling competent, worthy, valued, in control or fulfilled in some meaningful way.

Sensual pleasures encompass positive sensations experienced when feeling your own body move, respond or react, when feeling another body close to yours, when feeling the excitement and connection of sexual intimacy, when feeling your body totally relaxed, or when enjoying the wonderful things that you love to taste. The magic lies solely in absorbing yourself in the pleasurable sensations of these experiences.

Uplifting diversion includes activities that take you away from your normal chores through positive and absorbing diversion or through entertainment that you find relaxing or stimulating, such as reading, music, movies, TV, concerts, spectator sports/games, artistic performances or shopping. The magic lies in taking your mind to another place which absorbs you, lets your imagination wander or frees you, even momentarily.

Some magic moments . . .
a beaming smile
a warm hug
a positive comment
feeling appreciated
helping a friend
running through the woods
cycling into a refreshing breeze
paddling on an absolutely calm lake
a beautiful sunrise
a woodpecker making music on a hollow tree
listening to the sound of a flowing stream
a deer darting across a trail in the woods
finishing a chapter
thinking of new things
freshly squeezed orange juice
feeling strong
great sex
a hot shower
a relaxing massage
total connection

In my magic moments . . .
I feel loose, easy, light, in rhythm
I feel like a flowing stream
I feel like a soaring bird
I feel like a quiet lake
I feel totally connected to my body
    —running, paddling, lying in the sun
I feel sensual
I feel immersed in what I am doing

I feel alive, really alive
I feel bonded to my child, to my partner, to my interaction
I feel inseparably absorbed
I feel free
It's a very nice feeling

Taking Care of Yourself

When you enter the realm of parenting you step into a different world. There is less freedom, more demands and a heightened sense of responsibility. It is a true test of your patience, your capacity to give, and your ability to cope. With the additional demands it is a challenge for all parents to live balanced lives. The perspective you take into this world and carry around with you is critical for meeting this challenge successfully.

No matter how hard you try or how lofty your goals may be, there will be times when you are not great with your children and when they are not great with you. A realistic goal is to minimize those times and increase the times when you are at your best.

When I am less than my best with others it is almost always because I have been ignoring my own basic needs for rest, joy or personal space. I start to feel caged, trapped, restless, irritable or crabby. I overreact to little things that would normally never bother me. I don't like being this way, even for brief periods of time.

I've discovered that I always feel much better and interact much more effectively with children and others when I give myself little chunks of personal space. This means taking time for myself to do something that I want to do. Going for a walk or run in the countryside can do wonders for me. It gives me time alone with my thoughts and leaves me feeling alive, relaxed, refreshed and in control of some aspect of my life. We desperately need and greatly benefit from a little bit of personal space or magic just for ourselves, each day.

If we deny our basic needs for personal space, exercise,

rest, relaxation, healthy nutrition, meaningful pursuits, intimacy or pleasurable outings with others, we pay for it in the end, as do our loved ones. I'm sure you have sometimes felt that you spend so much time fulfilling the needs of others that you have no time or energy left for yourself. You are doing everything for others and nothing for yourself. It's a common trap that dedicated parents and teachers find themselves falling into. Being committed to your family and the quality of your work is very important; however, doing everything for others and nothing for yourself is not a healthy situation for anyone. It leaves you fatigued, irritable, stressed, sometimes sick and definitely less than your best.

You need to take care of you. No one else is likely to do that for you. If you are extremely busy, working outside the home, pulled in many directions at once, lack assistance at home, or are a single parent raising a child, it's even more important that you give yourself a breath of fresh air or a little time-out each day. It will lift you, make you feel better, stronger, happier and more balanced. It will insulate you from some of the ongoing stressors that confront you every day. It will allow you to live a healthier, more joyful and less stressed life.

What you choose to do with your time-out is totally up to you. The important thing is that you take time out, away from your work or chores, to enjoy the activities or pursuits that you find relaxing, stimulating or joyful. You may go walking, running, swimming, skiing, dancing, play a variety of sports, do fitness activities or visit with friends. You may garden, sew, listen to music, read, write, get a massage, lay outside on a rock in the sun, or simply find a place where you can enjoy some peace and quiet—all by yourself. This is your time to mellow out and dance with life.

You benefit from getting a break, doing something *you choose* to do, freeing yourself from other demands, and participating in something you enjoy. This leaves you feeling alive, relaxed and in control.

Physically active and physically relaxing time-outs are very effective for preventing and releasing stress. Both activity and relaxation serve to relieve stress, shift your thoughts away from stressful events and leave you in a more positive and relaxed state—mentally and physically.

Think into your own shoulders right now. Rotate them. Let them drop down a bit. Let them relax. Breathe easily and slowly. As you breathe out, think to yourself . . . relax. That's a good start. [If you are interested in learning to relax more fully see the audio tapes in the Resource Section at the back of this book.]

An important component of time-out activities is the sense of control it gives you over certain aspects of your life and the extent to which it makes you feel like a more complete person again. One mother put it quite simply, "When I'm dancing I forget that I'm a mother." It's important to "forget" that we are parents from time to time, because no matter how important parenting may be to us, we are never only parents, any more than we are only workers, executives, teachers or athletes. We are people first, with many of the same wants, needs and desires we had before we took on these roles. It's important and healthy to allow some of your other qualities to continue to live and grow.

Why don't you take a little time-out for yourself today? You'll feel better, look better, be better, love better, live better. If you think it's impossible because you don't have time, you're too busy, too tired, too exhausted, too many things to do, don't have any help, your partner does nothing or you are alone, think again. These are all good reasons but none good enough to justify not taking care of you. Let's assume I'm your doctor and I tell you that your life, or the life of your child, depends upon you taking at least 30 to 40 minutes a day just for you. Would it be possible then? Of course it would, because you would set it as a priority, schedule it and make it happen. That's exactly what you have to do, because the quality of lives *do* hang in the balance.

I am your doctor. I am giving you a prescription and I expect you to subscribe to it religiously.

Your prescription:

1. At least every other day (and more often when possible) take 30 to 40 minutes just for *you* (for example, go for a run, take part in an activity, have some fun, or do something you enjoy in a place or space of your choosing).

2. Every day take a five-minute break (and longer where possible) to relax *during* the day, in the eye of the hurricane.

3. Do it! Suspend thinking about why you can't do it. Figure out how you can—your life depends on it.

How to Get Yourself Out

If you are among the many parents at home who feel a need to get yourself out of the house for that much needed personal space, consider the following possibilities. Find another parent, or set of parents, with whom you feel compatible who have children of similar ages. Set up a rotation of responsibilities for caring for the children at specified times. For example, two or three parents might rotate so that each of the parents has full responsibility for all the children on selected days, half days or evenings of the week.

If you want to get a break for an hour or so during the day (for example to go for a walk or run), consider inviting another parent and child to come over for that hour, or taking your child over to their house for that hour, and then swapping roles during that day, or on alternative days. That way both parents and children get a break.

In the past I often arranged time-sharing lunches, brunches, picnics or suppers with other families who visited. During part of that time together, I would go for a run while one of them took care of the children, and then they would go out for a run while I took over child-care duties. We all had some personal activity time and some time together.

When there are two parents in a household, you have the additional option of directly involving your partner in time sharing so that you have some personal time when your partner comes home from a day of work outside the home. Other options are to hire a good part-time caregiver to come into your home on certain days, or to take your children to a well-run play-school for limited time periods while you fulfill some of your own personal needs. If you have any money it's a great way to spend it because it so directly effects your health and sanity.

If you decide that you really need time for you, and set it as a priority, you can devise a way to make it happen. In order to parent, teach, run and write, I figured out all sorts of shared parenting arrangements with other parents, friends and family members. I also learned to make personal use of the times of the day when most of the world sleeps (very early in the morning or late at night).

As your children get older, your options become a lot easier and more plentiful. The children become more independent and have more of their own activities that they want to pursue. They can immerse themselves in play, games, sticker or stamp collections, creative activities, books, projects or a good video while you do a few of the personal things that are important to you.

Getting Out With Your Children

One morning I was fed up with being in the house. It was pretty obvious because I was beginning to feel irritable and overreact to things. The house was a mess, and one of my daughter's friends who had slept over was constantly demanding attention. I needed some space. At that point I would have loved to run away for an hour and return with a new perspective. But I couldn't arrange it that day, and the children were too young to be left on their own. So we all bundled up and went outside onto a frozen lake. We pushed a ball around with brooms, slid on the ice, built some snow things and breathed in some fresh, crisp air. When we came back in for lunch, I felt rejuvenated . . . more like my normal self . . . and so did the children.

For those times when it is difficult or impossible to get a break on your own, think of ways you can do stimulating things that you like to do, together with your children. Going for walks to parks, beaches, lakes or outdoor markets, all have the capacity to shift your focus and free you and your children from being cooped up inside the house for long hours.

Discover joyful activities that free both you and your children at the same time. When my daughter first began riding her two-wheel bicycle on her own, we would go outside together and I would run while she rode. We both experienced a sense of freedom and joy during the activity. Over the years, various activities in outdoor settings have provided this mutual sense of connection, freedom and joy.

I love to be outside in natural settings. It lifts me immensely and provides a great opportunity for children to play in creative ways, with movement, earth, sand, rocks, water, leaves and sticks. I can relax and enjoy myself and be comforted by the fact that the children have plenty of options for positive exploration and playful interaction.

Parents who enjoy physical activities have discovered some interesting ways to continue to engage in them with young children. These include jogging while pushing their child in a stroller, cross-country skiing while pulling their child, all bundled up, in a sled called a pulka, walking or hiking while carrying their children in Snugglies or backpacks, and cycling on bike paths with children in special trailers, strollers or carrier seats. For parents who are attracted to more organized options, there are parent-tot programs for fitness, swimming, aerobics, and various other activities where parents can exercise or play, while their children play with other children. There are also parent-child programs where parents and children can take lessons or do activities together.

Sharing the Load

The first six to eight months following a birth are probably the most difficult in terms of adjusting to new demands. A large part of the difficulty relates to the baby's interference with normal sleeping patterns. There is also a tremendous adaptation in daily lifestyle for the primary parent, as well as some significant changes for the parenting partner.

Giving birth is an exhilarating and exhausting process, mentally and physically. It is an intense ultra-marathon that is more taxing than even the most strenuous athletic event. A new mother needs rest and support to regain her energy. This is greatly facilitated when the parenting partner, or another supportive person, takes care of the normal household chores (for example, making food, doing dishes, cleaning house, making beds, shopping, etc.) while she tries to recoup her energy and take care of the baby's essential needs. Complete support during recovery should be provided for at least a week or two. Forever after, the load should be shared by partners.

The most obvious initial sharing requirement is sharing the right to sleep. In the beginning it is common to be wakened several times during the night. Often it seems to occur just after you have fallen into a deep sleep. There are times where you might feel like you are in some kind of interrogation chamber. You are dead tired, and every time you begin to drift off to sleep it's as if someone slaps you or splashes water in your face. This can be very draining for both parents, especially if you are a light sleeper. For a woman who has just finished the intense physical and emotional marathon of birth it can be especially exhausting.

One solution which may help to avoid continued overload on any one parent, is to take turns with fulfilling the baby's needs during the night. "Tonight you sleep as much as possible; it's *my* responsibility to respond if the baby cries. I will provide the hugging and consoling, diaper changing and bottle feeding." Those mothers who are providing the wonderful gift of breast feeding may not be able to sleep too long before having to get up and feed the baby or express their milk, but even a little extra time or support helps.

If one partner is inclined to say "I have to work tomorrow, I need my sleep," I assure you that the person working inside the home also needs sleep. Having experienced full-time work inside the home as well as outside, it is clear to me that the person inside the home has more constant demands, and needs sleep at least as much as the person who leaves the house in the morning and returns at the end of the day.

When going through difficult phases, some parents may be inclined to feel that it will continue forever. What did I get myself into? Am I ever going to have a full night's sleep again? Will we ever go out again? Am I ever going to be able to relax?

But it doesn't last forever! Things get better and better. You have more and more fun with your child, and you figure out ways to make things work. Before you know it, to your amazement, your child is in pre-school, then elementary school, then secondary school. Soon you will be looking back, telling others that the phases move very quickly. The all-consuming demands on your time lessen as your children become more and more independent. Time frames are altered dramatically the day your children go to school. At that point your children are gone all day long, and if you're anything like me, you will be wishing you had more time with them.

Helping Spouses

It is a great gift for the whole family when parents share fully in the child-rearing process. If your spouse is not willing to be part of the shared parenting process you are essentially a single parent. The only difference is that instead of having one person to take care of, you have two—one who is toilet trained and one who is not.

I don't mind cooking, cleaning, shopping, washing, etc., for a person who is incapable of doing it. I even enjoy parts of it because I am fulfilling a real need. But if I do it all by myself for a fully capable adult for more than a few weeks I begin to resent it.

I learned a lot about males and females when I became a full-time parent. Some of the males who visited, with their wives or without them, did virtually nothing to help and expected others to serve them. Some of them would probably starve or at least trim their waistline considerably if someone didn't make supper for them every night. If they brought the plate they used (only theirs) from the table to the edge of the sink, they considered it an absolute fulfillment of all their helping duties. They seemed entirely oblivious to the fact that there is a process of food preparation that begins long before eating, and a process of cleaning up (pots, pans, dishes, utensils, tables, countertops, etc.) which extends far beyond dessert. The women are entirely different. They help without ever being asked to help. They understand that there is a job that has to be done which is not necessarily my job. To be fair to men, I have noted that in recent years more and more men who visit chip in and help in a meaningful way. (I don't know if that is because they are getting better at helping or I'm getting better at selecting helpful people to invite.)

Some partners need help in understanding what is really involved in taking care of a family and running a household. When there are two parents in residence, it is important that both accept that it is not fair or in the best interests of either parent or the family for one to be expected to carry the full load.

With some partners, open discussions about feelings, responsibilities and needs, along with providing some selected reading can help. For others, nothing is likely to be as effective as letting them independently take on the full parenting role for a period of time. A week or two of doing everything usually results in a substantial increase in understanding, a month or two will suffice for a more complete appreciation of what is entailed, and anything longer than that will likely ensure that they either automatically pitch in to help, or leave. Once worthy partners have lived the "doing everything" role, they won't feel good about themselves unless they do their share, especially when they are helping people they love and care about. We all have to realize that no one is master, no one is slave. We are partners in this process. No one's life, work or free time is more important than another's.

Staying Positive With Yourself

Perspectives

If you look for the positives in life
you will find opportunities in everything,
even within problems.

If you look for the negatives in life
you will find problems in everything,
even within opportunities

One view frees you to live joyfully,
the other imprisons you.

You create your own view.
Choose it wisely.

You have the capacity to remain positive with yourself most of the time, even in situations that you currently view as negative or stressful. Something is only stressful if you allow it to upset you. Otherwise it is simply something that happens as you go through your day. You can choose to be upset by it or to not be, to dwell on it or to let it go. You don't lose your *capacity* to be positive with yourself or with others because of the little hassles you face. *You do allow yourself to lose the perspective that enables you to stay positive and interact effectively.*

You have three choices in dealing with a hassle.

1. You can let it keep bothering you, which doesn't help anyone.

2. You can put it aside or temporarily "shelve it," which makes great sense for things not very important, things beyond your control, or for things you don't feel like dealing with right now.

3. You can immediately attempt to remedy or correct the situation that is bothering you. This makes sense if it is within your control, if others are ready to listen, or if you feel it is worth expending the necessary energy at the moment.

If you are faced with a multitude of demands or little hassles over a short period of time, which is common in parenting and teaching situations, and you let yourself get upset over all of them, it won't be long before you are mentally and physically exhausted. It takes a lot of energy to react in an emotional way to all of these potentially stressful situations. Over a period of weeks, months or years, if you continue to react by upsetting yourself or worrying, there is a good chance you will end up feeling run-down or sick. Constantly reacting in a stressful way not only affects your mood, it lowers your resistance. This can be detrimental to you, your performance, your health and your capacity to care for others.

You will cope better with stress if you are well rested. So if you are expecting a tough day or week, use your ingenuity to find a way to get some rest. Where possible take a little time out to relax before, during and after stressful encounters. When living through stressful circumstances, set some simple daily goals, or plan part of your day *for you*, so you have a sense of control over at least some aspect of what you do that day.

Sometimes it's helpful to step back and look at the things you get upset about, as if observing from a distance. Most of them are little things that usually get worked out within a short period of time. They really aren't worth wasting your energy getting all stressed out about. There is no advantage in panicking over every little current, wave or ripple. Ride them through. Save your energy for the big ones that really count.

Let's say some little screw-up or hassle is beginning to bug you. As soon as you begin to feel it, before it gets too big, take a deep breath, exhale slowly, and say to yourself, "Relax . . . this is not worth getting upset about. I would prefer that it wasn't happening, but it's not that big a deal. It doesn't have to bother me. It's not worth upsetting myself about. "Shelve it," "tree it" or "tea it."

Little things tend to bug you more when you are already keyed up because you don't take the time to see them for what they really are—little, insignificant things. Your challenge is to keep them in perspective. Something as simple as a tea break can help bring things back into perspective. A friend who is the mother of three, often uses tea breaks to settle things down and regain perspective. When recounting how she dealt with a little hassle, she smiled and said, "I tead it."

Let's say that you're on your way home from work or shopping and you are stewing about a hassle that happened while you were out. You know that it won't help you to continue to dwell on it when you arrive home, and you want to arrive in good spirits to play with your children or snuggle with your mate. It would have been nice if everything had gone smoothly, but it didn't, and you can't change that now. What you *can* control is how you react, what you do with yourself and how you respond to your family.

On your way home, commit yourself to getting back on a positive track by changing mental channels from negative to positive. Begin to prepare yourself to arrive in a manner that will be of most value to you, your children and your partner. Think of past positive experiences, or uplifting things you would like to do when you get home. Let them run through your mind. Either in the car, or as you walk up to your home, press your hand hard against some object, for example the steering wheel, a tree, the outside wall, or the door handle. At the same time think to yourself, "leave your hassle here," "wheel it", "tree it", "change channels." Then smile and say to yourself, "I am going to spend the next half hour doing something I really enjoy doing—relaxing, playing with my children or playing with my mate. I am going to get the most out of the rest of the day." If a hassle is really worthy of your life energy, discuss it with your loved ones later on at an appropriate time, and consider specifically how you will deal with it. If it's not that important forget it now *and* later.

When I'm on my way to work I begin to prepare for what I want to do there. I think about it, review it in my mind and plan what I want to do. Once I leave work I begin to prepare for what I want to do at home. I change channels. I turn off the "at work" channel and turn on the "at home" channel. Tuning into the right channel at the right time is what allows us to be more effective in our work and more balanced in our living.

There is a hill not far from my home that I use as my final reminder to shift gears or change channels. Every day on my way home I drive up that hill, and as I come over the top I breathe out, relax my body, smile and think, "it's great to be home. I'm going to enjoy the rest of this day." In my mind I run through activities that I might enjoy doing on my own (if no one is home) or together with my loved ones. I try to get myself into a playful mood by thinking about playful things, especially if it's been a heavy day. Upon arrival at home, if any family members are there, I devote myself totally to family contact for at least the first 15 or 20 minutes. I greet them, hug them, ask about their day, play with them, show them that I'm delighted to see them. They are all that exist in my life at that time. I am truly happy to be home.

My hill reminds me to "relax" and leave work, hassles, fatigue or bad feelings behind. If I have difficulty shifting focus I often repeat the words "change channels," or "forget it and focus" several times in a row. This is my reminder to forget it and focus on what I want to do now. This is all aimed at helping me relax, carry good energy, get into something I enjoy, be "all here" and enjoy the time I have. It reminds me that I am in control of my thoughts, my focus and the rest of my day.

To stay on track or get back on track quickly:

- *Commit yourself to remain positive.* A strong positive focus protects you from negative moods and potential hassles.
- *Remind yourself to keep things in perspective.* Children do not set out intentionally to restrict your freedom, interrupt your sleep or cause problems. They are just exploring, developing their skills and following their own internal rhythms. They are still beginners at comprehending rules, understanding others, coping and communicating.
- *Get yourself into a positive state of mind at the beginning of the day.* Before the day starts, while you are still in bed, think about doing some things that are most likely to make you feel good and keep you in a positive frame of mind. Focus on doing some of those things during the day.
- *Look for advantages in every possible situation,* even under what might normally be considered less than ideal conditions. Look for reasons why you can still be positive, confident and optimistic. There is no advantage in dragging yourself down or wasting your energy trying to control things that are totally beyond your control. Do what you can do . . . draw out the constructive lessons . . . and move forward.
- *Remind yourself that simple mishaps or potential hassles do not have to bother you.* You can refuse to get caught up in them. You can let them go. Things may happen that you do not like or appreciate, but you control how you react to them. Don't compound the problem by wasting your good energy on things which make you or your

loved ones feel worse, rather than better. Look for something positive. Look for your own strength.

- When things don't go as well as you would like with your children, partner or work, *draw out the lessons, learn for the next time, and refocus into a more positive state of mind.* Take a time out, find your own space, regroup your thoughts, do something you enjoy, focus on doing something that is within your control.

- *Absorb yourself in the simple joys and magic moments of life.* Refuse to waste your time on irrelevant hassles. You will then have more energy for enjoying the good things that you do have, more in general to give others, and more time for living the joyful moments of life.

During difficult or challenging times you need healthy breaks, absorbing distractions and times for yourself to live, laugh, and have fun—even though these may be of short duration. When facing major setbacks all you can do is everything humanly possible to resolve the situation in a constructive way. You can share your genuine feelings and concerns. You can remind yourself that part of this is out of your control. You can give up the need or obsession to control what is beyond your control.

A sensitive and caring woman who was trying to cope with some major personal losses shared with me some absorbing focuses that worked best for her to change channels or shift focus. "There are two best things that help me shift focus, no matter how horribly things are going—a good long run and good sex, and not necessarily in that order." Positive, absorbing focuses that are uplifting for you can provide a lift at any time and may be particularly important when experiencing major setbacks or losses.

After each and every day—good or not so good—be proud of your efforts and what you have done well, draw out the positive lessons . . . and then start fresh. Every day is a new day with new opportunities.

Growing From Your Own Experiences

The wonderful part of being human is that you have
the capacity to control your own thinking and thereby
direct the course of your own life.

One of the best ways to become a more competent parent, teacher or performer in any pursuit is to look closely at your good days and not so good days. This allows you to draw out positive lessons from your own experiences. If you act upon these lessons you will have more "good days" and be more consistent at being your best.

In my attempt to become a better parent and teacher, I got into the habit of thinking about what I did well, and where I could have been better, as each day came to a close. Reflecting on my good days, and on what I did well, enabled me to better understand what helped me be the best parent and teacher I could be. It taught me how I could be this way on a more consistent basis.

I also learned a lot from reflecting upon my worst days, and then did everything in my power to prevent them from reoccurring. There haven't been many days where I have felt totally negative or ineffective as a parent, but those few times left me feeling very inadequate. I always tried to draw out lessons from those less-than-best experiences to set the conditions for being more positive, happier with myself and better in the future.

I recall one particular morning that was not great. It was a morning when I was feeling the need for a little bit of extra space. I had not gotten out of the house the previous day and I was faced with a few unexpected hassles this particular morning. In addition, the arrangements I had made for a short break had fallen through. I wasn't in my most positive frame of mind. However, it was a beautiful morning when my daughter's cousin arrived for the day, and the three of us went outside. They were both three and a half years old at the time. They played in the grass, bounced on an in-ground trampoline, played under the trees and threw things in the water. I was sitting on a picnic table not far away, thinking to myself, "It's a beautiful morning, I'm in a beautiful setting, with two beautiful kids—why am I not feeling more appreciative and happy?"

Instead of shifting into a playful channel, as I usually do, I was dwelling on missing my run and thinking about not having enough personal space for me. This way of thinking prevented me from being fully involved with the children and the beauty around me. I didn't bounce on the trampoline with them or skip rocks in the water, or play with them like I normally do.

I was physically present but mentally absent . . . here but not here. Not a great place to be! At one point, while playing next to the water, the children got their feet and pants wet. The water was extremely cold because the ice had just left the lake, so it wouldn't have been wise to stand in the water too long. But it was a very warm day, and getting their feet or pants wet wouldn't really do any harm. Normally in a situation like this I step back and ask myself, "does it really make a big difference?" They're having a lot of fun, they're exploring, learning, being creative and interacting with each other and nature. Is it *really* necessary to interfere? Usually the answer is no! There is rarely a good reason to interfere with normal exploratory play.

This day I didn't do that. Instead of sitting back calmly, observing and asking myself these questions, I let my negative thoughts interfere with their enjoyment. "Look at your pants—the bottoms are all wet!" In retrospect I wondered, where did that come from? Give me a break Orlick, so what!

Who cares? Pants dry in the sun! Anyway, what's more important—dry pants or happy, creative children?

I suggested that we do a job together that I needed to do, which I thought they would also enjoy. I had to move a floating raft about 16 meters from one point to another. So I got out a paddle for each of us, and we all got on the raft and started paddling. They were really enjoying themselves. But I was far too task oriented and much less tolerant than usual. Instead of enjoying the process of paddling, and gradually trying to get the raft moving in the right direction, I wanted to get from point A to point B without delay. "Ok, men, let's get the job done here and don't screw around; I don't care if you are only three years old." I didn't actually say that, but that's the way I was acting.

In reality, it didn't make any difference which way they paddled because they put so little power into their stroke anyway. I yelped at them when there was no need to yelp. The only purpose it served was to make me realize how negative I was being. We finally got the dock over to point B and I managed a few positive words. The day wasn't a total disaster, because I didn't do any irreparable damage, but I broke a few little balloons within people I love. And I really didn't like the way I had acted.

When I sat back and evaluated that day, I was able to pull out some important lessons. First, I know I function better if I've had some space for me, so I had to make more reliable arrangements for that to happen, *in advance* whenever possible.

Second, my space *did* come later that day . . . so if I don't get my space when expected (for example, in the morning), I should remember that it may be only delayed . . . not entirely eliminated. "Don't needlessly upset yourself; you might prefer some space (or a run) right now . . . but it's not that big a deal. You can get into what you are doing now, and get your personal space later today, or tomorrow."

Third, I had to develop a strategy to prevent this kind of thing from happening again, for example, remind myself that the children have nothing to do with this. They have no control over my lack of space. Don't take it out on them. Lighten up. Put this in perspective . . . it's a small thing, let's not blow it out of proportion. Don't hurt the ones you love. Look for positive things. Be here. Be positive. Look for the magic moments.

The very next day I had a super day with the children, largely because I took the time to reflect and decided to do some things to prevent a reoccurrence of the previous day. I got up early and wrote for about an hour (actually about this incident) while everyone else was still sleeping. This helped me to clarify the issue in my own mind and also left me feeling I had accomplished something. I felt good about having reflected on what had happened and also felt good about having done some writing. As soon as my parenting partner got up, I went for a run. That felt good too—something for me.

After my partner left, while I was making breakfast for the children, I thought to myself, "Today I'm going to try to totally avoid saying no, unless there is a real reason for a no." A legitimate reason for "no" would include a *real* possibility of physical injury, hurting another person or destruction of some very important property. I committed myself to avoid unnecessary "no"s, before the day got going. It turned out to be a wonderful day.

The first event that could have evoked a negative response was when one of the children kicked over a kitchen chair next to the table. I delayed for a moment before responding—long enough to breathe in one long, slow, deep breath and to then slowly breathe out. I reminded myself to "stay positive." I calmly picked up the chair and respectfully explained that it probably wasn't a good idea to kick the chair over because when falling down it might break an arm. I pointed out the arms on the chair and touched them.

I suggested an alternative possibility, which allowed the children to maintain a sense of personal control. "If you want to push the chair over onto the ground, you can do it slowly so we don't break any arms." Together we gently lowered the chair to the ground. "Then you can use the chair as your fort, bus, airplane or whatever you want." They readily accepted that explanation and treated the chair respectfully.

During the day I played with the children and followed their pace. I also gave them ample time to play on their own, watching from a safe distance. I only interfered with a "no" once during that whole day and it was done gently, respectfully and with concern for the children. This occurred when they were outside playing in the water. I became concerned that they were getting too cold. I did not interfere with them taking off their shoes, socks and long pants, and wading knee deep into the cold water with squeals of joy. But after a little while, when their legs began to get red I stepped in, dried them off, dressed them, explained that their legs needed to warm up and suggested we walk to a special place to warm things up.

On many occasions I have had the opportunity to learn from observing good parents on their good days and not so good days. On one such occasion a parent decided to prepare a picnic and take her two children (three and four years old) on a walk to a special picnic spot. She loved to do this and so did her children . . . so she began to prepare. They got everything ready and put their picnic goodies in little packsacks for each child to carry. Everything was going well until it was time to put the children's shoes on and actually get out the door.

Little Mary wanted to wear her sandals. Her mother wanted her to wear running shoes. The mother explained that she thought it would be better to wear running shoes. Mary insisted on putting on her sandals. The mother left the room and when she returned found that Mary had proceeded with putting on her sandals—and they were on the wrong feet. In a stern voice the mother said, "They're on the wrong feet— change them." Mary replied, "It doesn't matter."

Finally the mom got mad and yelled, "I don't want to spend

all morning getting shoes on. I want to go on the picnic!" As she said this, she slammed her hand hard on the floor. Mary was startled. She began to cry and ran towards her room. Her mom intercepted Mary as she headed for her room, picked her up, slid her onto her knee and changed her shoes to the "correct" feet. She said, "I don't want to hear any more whining or crying," and quickly exited the house with both children.

Upon reflection she did not feel good about her actions. She thought about how useless it was to "blow up" at Mary. So while walking down the road, she spoke calmly to her, apologized, and explained that she was only trying to help her make the best choice (for shoes). She took Mary's hand in her own and said, "I'm not perfect and sometimes I have bad days and sometimes I get angry too." Mary seemed to understand.

After this explanation and sharing of feelings, everyone was calmer and feeling better. Being outside, walking hand-in-hand, also helped. The children quickly absorbed themselves in play, and the mother allowed herself to enjoy the remaining moments of the day.

If you are not feeling good about yourself on a particular day, or if you have not made arrangements to do something for yourself for several days, then your capacity to serve others is greatly diminished. This is what had happened with this mother on this particular day, and she was simply less tolerant than usual as a result. Whenever possible, plan to meet your needs for personal space *before* you reach a state of low tolerance. This will set the stage for more good days.

The day after the sandals incident I had an opportunity to play with little Mary. In a nonchalant way I asked her why she liked wearing her sandals better than her running shoes. Mary said, "because I can tie these up, all by myself." There were two little buckles on her sandals which she could buckle and unbuckle easily. With her running shoes, she still had to depend upon someone else to tie them up properly. Mary made her shoe choice because she wanted to wear something over which she could exercise personal control, especially in that she would be undoing and doing them up often around the water at the picnic site.

Over the years I have often found good reasons for children's choices. Before we unknowingly or unwittingly interfere with what might be a very reasoned choice from the child's eyes, it's often helpful to ask why, in a respectful way. "I'm interested in why you made that choice. Why do you think you prefer that one (or those shoes)?"

Eric, an eight-year-old, was preparing to go on a little vacation with his father. Eric was very excited about the trip and they spent much of the day packing together. Shortly before they had to leave for the airport, Eric started pulling things out of his bag and getting new things to bring. His dad's patience ran thin at this point. He harped at Eric about always leaving things to the last second, not telling him earlier that he had wanted these additional things, and complaining about spending his whole day packing for his son. He was still barking at Eric when they got in the car to leave. Eric lowered his head and looked at the floor. When his dad finally stopped harping, in a very quiet voice Eric said, "I feel so bad about myself."

At that instant Eric's father felt the impact of his negative comments. He apologized to Eric, explained that he had been rushing all morning to get things ready and had run out of good energy. He said, "This isn't something that should make you feel bad about yourself." Both he and Eric were upset with themselves for starting the trip on a negative note.

In reflecting on it later, Eric's dad said to me, "I made a bigger deal of it than it had to be. If I had stopped and listened to myself bitching, I would have been disgusted with myself. It was as if I wanted to hurt him or see him punished." From Eric's perspective there were simply a couple of important things that he had forgotten about until the last minute. Once he remembered, he wanted to get them and bring them along. On the vacation, they did in fact turn out to be important additions.

It would have been better on Eric's feelings, as well as his father's, to say something like, "OK, Eric, let's get those things quickly because we both really want to get going on our trip." Then later on, when they were both relaxed, Eric and his dad could have drawn out some positive lessons for next time. For example, "Next time, let's try to think of what we need to take earlier, and remind each other of what we need to take." Where the goal is to have a child learn something from the experience, a clear statement of where he could function better for the future is usually sufficient. There's no advantage in putting him down or punishing him.

The problem with harping at children for what we perceive as imperfections, errors or omissions is that they end up feeling bad about themselves, as people. If we do it often enough they come to view themselves, in their totality, as bad, incompetent, dumb, irresponsible and unworthy of love.

We start with these beautiful little people who are as open as the day is long. If we shower them with our good parts and good days they blossom. If we expose them to too many of our bad days, or our incompetencies, they wilt away and die inside. If for no other reason, you have to take care of yourself and your own needs so that you have more good days, in order to give your best to your children.

Setting the Stage for Good Days

One of the best ways to set the stage for good days is to take a little time to reflect upon what allows you to have "good days." You can begin right now by thinking through the following questions, and perhaps writing down your responses.

1. What sorts of things give you a lift, make you feel good, relax you, absorb you in a positive way, or make you feel happy to be alive? Do you spend enough time doing these things? If not, what can you do to make sure you do some of these things more often?

2. What personal needs of yours have to be respected for you to feel good about yourself? What can you do to help ensure that these personal needs are respected?

3. On your good days, when you are in your best frame of mind with your children and other loved ones, what do you think contributes to it? For example, are you well rested, have you had some free time, are you feeling appreciated?

4. On good days how is your positive frame of mind reflected in your interactions with your children? For example, what do you do that is different from other days? Do you communicate with them in a more respectful way? Are you more open with your affection, more involved with them or more tolerant of their actions? How can you interact with them in this way more frequently?

5. When you are in a less-than-best frame of mind, for example, more irritable, crabby or negative than usual, what do you think contributes to it?

6. Have you noticed any patterns which precede or make you more susceptible to a good frame of mind versus a bad frame of mind? For example, is it related to personal time for yourself, or support from others, stress, pressure, fatigue, exercise, relaxation, rest or nutrition?

7. When you slip into a less-than-best frame of mind, have you ever been able to shift gears or change channels to get yourself back into a more positive frame of mind? If yes, how have you done this?

8. How can you respect and follow the patterns that have allowed you to feel and act positively in the past? How

can you set the stage for having good days more often in the future?

Once you have thought through these questions, your challenge is to put some of your answers into action. If you commit yourself to turn your reflections into positive action it will lead to more personal growth for you, and a greater sense of fulfillment within your children and relationships.

Quality Time Zones

When selecting activities that can lift your day, or people who can lift your life, it is most important that you feel good within yourself when you are engaged in this activity or in the presence of this person. Time alone or with others becomes quality time when it makes you feel good about the connection you experience and good about yourself.

Quality time in any domain requires a total connection with what you are doing. It is a time of full focus. When sharing quality time with a loved one, the total focus is on interacting with that person. Nothing else in the world exists, beyond that experience, for that period of time. You are totally, positively connected—listening, absorbing, reflecting, talking, playing, moving, laughing, loving, experiencing. You are not thinking about work, watching TV, listening to the radio, reading, or worrying about the past or future demands. This is a special time that engenders feelings of connection, acceptance, love, importance and caring within both people.

Quality Time Zones for Growth Within Families

Parents, children, families and relationships, have the best chance of fully developing when five "life-time" zones are respected:

1. Time for you (for your own personal nourishment).

2. Time for you alone with your child (one-on-one special time together).

3. Time for you alone with your partner (one-on-one time when you both still have positive energy).

4. Time for your family unit together.

5. Time for your child to play with other children.

Time For You

Making time for your own personal space and personal growth, needs to be given priority because it allows you to survive as a dedicated parent and grow as an individual person. When you feel good *about you*, others will also feel better *with you*. You need time away from the demands or dictates of others, either with friends or by yourself. Choose something to do for you that takes you away from obligations, provides positive diversion, allows for reflection or stimulates personal growth. Choose something that carries you into another realm, something that absorbs you, frees you, nurtures your soul or lifts your spirits, even for short periods of time.

One-on-One Time With Your Child

Something magical happens between a parent and child when just the two of you share quality time together. When you are alone together and give children your full attention they become more responsive, helpful, cuddly and openly loving. The connected feelings and sense of security experienced through this close, uninterrupted contact is difficult to generate any other way. Plus, it gives you an opportunity to really enjoy your child, to learn from him/her and become one with him/her, for at least a portion of the day. Spending one-on-one time with your child will not guarantee perfect harmony, but it will guarantee the sharing of magic moments. An absence of this one-on-one time together will result in less harmony, less intimacy and less joy in the relationship.

First you need a commitment to spend uninterrupted time

together. Then you can begin to work on ensuring that the time together is of high quality. *Time is life.* Time spent in one place is life away from another. Your greatest challenge is to balance your time wisely, giving or working enough to feel good about what you are doing, but not so much that it swallows you or leaves feelings of emptiness within you or your loved ones.

One-on-One Time With Your Partner

This is a zone that can easily slide or take a backseat to work or the children. It is often the last area we address for improvement. Initially, as a dedicated parent, you center on fulfilling your child's needs. Before long, you begin to realize that you also need some space, time alone or time with other pursuits to feel like a more complete person again. You may find that personal space for yourself and invest in some precious one-on-one time with your child, and still be in a situation where you and your partner have very little quality time alone together. It is very difficult to maintain a close connection with an adult partner when you don't do anything really pleasurable together.

Let's assume that two parents share the child rearing responsibilities. She is responsible for being with the children on weekdays while her partner works and plays, or some combination thereof. By the time he gets home, eats supper, bathes the kids and reads to them while she cleans up and does dishes, she's tired. After the kids go to bed, she doesn't have a lot of physical or mental energy left for playing or love-making, or being happy or sad with him about his happy or not so happy day. So she does a few quiet things around the house and goes to bed, because she's exhausted and the kids get up early. Remember she shares the early morning hours with them. If the roles are reversed, by the time she gets home from work at supper time, he is tired, exhausted, wants to do something for himself or go to bed.

There may be a feeling of mutual support and appreciation

for parts of the contribution each parent is making, but also a sense of ships passing in the night, or the changing of the guard. One arrives to relieve the other, and the other leaves to do his or her own thing. If both parents are working or there is only one parent doing everything, it can become even more challenging and exhausting.

Before you fully realize it, you may slip into a pattern which is respectful of the children, good for your own personal space, but not so good for your relationship with your partner. If you're not careful, this pattern can easily wind along for years, ungluing the intimacy in your relationship. Patterns set are sometimes difficult to break.

When was the last time you and your partner had some quality time together, alone? Does it happen often enough? When was the last time you both played hooky from work or chores solely to spend the morning or afternoon frolicking together? Many parents have not fully lived a day of love-making or just lying around enjoying each other, since before they became parents. They haven't taken the time for long walks, meaningful talks, picnics or been playful together in a very long time. Perhaps you have felt this ungluing of your relationship or even mentioned it in passing.

All relationships benefit from uninterrupted physical, spiritual or emotional intimacy at times when both partners are fully awake and both are carrying good, positive energy. Have you taken the time to ensure this happens?

Think of the things you used to do together that gave you the most pleasure, joy or sense of connection. Write those things down on separate lists so you can share them with each other. These don't have to be big things. Look for the little things that make you or your partner feel good, special, loved, beautiful, appreciated or positively connected. See if you can find some things on your lists that will lift you both. Then set some times to experience these pleasureful events together. Write your preferences, share them and act on them.

There *are* times when you can do this, if you decide that

the quality of your relationship is important enough. You can plan to share pleasurable time together during certain day-time or evening hours by arranging, or taking advantage of your children's involvement in, activities with friends, relatives, neighbors or other caregivers. You can squeeze in some special times during pre-school or school hours. As your children get older there is potentially more time to be together with your partner. However, it still requires planning and a commitment to specific, positive action, to become an ongoing reality.

Mutually joyful one-on-one time with your partner is an area which warrants attention in all relationships. If you do not pay attention to maintaining quality time within this relationship, much of its original reason for being will dissolve or slip away. Only if you both allocate good time and energy to this relationship along the way, will it continue to grow now and in the future, long after the children have left and started their own families.

Close loving relationships develop and grow when there is a special sense of inter-dependency. Each person needs and depends upon the other person for certain feelings and experiences. You feel special, better or enriched in the presence of this person or when engaged in certain experiences with this person. They bring out special, positive feelings in you that you cannot experience alone. They make you feel good about you. Both children and adults gain immensely from these kinds of relationships.

Self-sufficiency is important for individual growth, but it is inter-dependency that creates bonds between people and intimacy in relationships. If this sense of inter-dependency or shared positive experience is absent or lost because one or both partners immerse themselves in work or other independent activities, and thereby exclude the other, then the essence of the close, loving relationship is lost. Some of the original joys you experienced together must be maintained or replaced by other joys, if the relationship is to survive. There has to be a reason to be together, or a sense of each person being desired, important or needed within the relationship.

With our children, we know they need us. We respond to their needs, they respond to our love, and that creates a bond. Perhaps one of the reasons we grow to need them is because they need us. The closest relationships develop in situations where we feel a need for another person and feel needed and appreciated in return. When we respond to each other's needs with emotional support (love and hugs) rather than just intellectual support (technical information or instructions), bonds are strengthened.

If we feel that our partner has no real appreciation for us, or that he or she prefers to spend his/her time elsewhere, it is difficult to maintain a strong commitment or intimate bond. This often occurs when we fail to spend quality time together or spend the time we do have arguing or putting each other down rather than doing the things that lift us.

In virtually all situations, we are more committed, feel better and contribute more when we feel respected, needed, appreciated, valued and wanted. The best way to help people, young and old, to know they are appreciated is to share pleasurable time with them, share feelings with them, express appreciation for their good qualities and acknowledge some of the many important contributions they make.

You can't create or maintain a sense of mutual love and appreciation without shared experiences. That normally requires time together. You need time together to be yourself, to discuss feelings, to share needs and dreams, to provide support, and perhaps most of all to absorb yourselves in simple pleasures. If you are never together, or rarely take time to share mutually pleasurable experiences, then you may easily grow to believe that there is no personal need for the other person, apart from serving a mechanical, monetary or service role.

Emotional bonding begins by feeling a natural connection with someone. It grows from feeling wanted and needed, or from feeling stronger, more complete or more fulfilled *with* this person than without. Natural communication and shared pleasurable experiences are important parts of this development. Both partners must be willing to create shared positive experiences and to communicate in a cooperative and respectful way.

Listening and accepting without judging is a big part of creating bonds between people. The moment communication becomes judgmental or a competition against another for dominance, power, control, scoring or winning, it cuts off the sharing of real feelings and becomes counterproductive. An important goal of meaningful communication is a deeper understanding and acceptance of another person's qualities, perspectives and needs. This can lead to true understanding, genuine problem solving and an improved shared living situation, with each partner feeling better about himself, herself and the relationship.

At times communication, or lack of it, may also lead to accepting that some people just aren't made to live or work together in harmony. They (or their circumstances) just don't fit in certain ways that are critical to the growth of these individuals or the relationship. Sometimes the uneasiness, distress or distancing experienced is a stimulus to rekindle some of the original joys in the relationship; other times the difficulties have profound roots and are a legitimate calling to move on to something that will be much less stressful and much more deeply satisfying. What we are really looking for in an interpersonal relationship is a soul mate, "someone to whom we feel profoundly connected, as though the communicating and communing that take place between us were not the product of intentional efforts, but rather a divine grace" (Moore, T. (1994) *Soul Mates: Honoring the Mysteries of Love and Relationships*. New York, N.Y.: Harper Collins).

The Fit of Relationships—One day while I was stacking a large pile of firewood , I sat down for a rest and looked very closely at the wood in front of me. I viewed those split pieces of wood like individuals within relationships. I began taking out pairs of wood and placing them together to see how well they fit. It was clear that some pairs fit together naturally, while others had big gaps between them. To close some of those big gaps would require quite a bit of slicing and carving, changing the essential make-up of at least one and perhaps both of those pieces. Otherwise they would never really fit snuggly together. When two pieces of wood had small gaps between them, a little bit of adjusting allowed them to fit snuggly together. Neither piece had to change its essential shape or essence.

People within all relationships have some gaps between them and experience some conflicts. However, the chances for harmony and a natural quality connection that endures are greatly facilitated when two people begin with a natural fit in terms of grain, texture and essential values. A "fit" in terms of basic human values, love and respect is very important. There is also the fit of feelings. Do the feelings flow in positive directions? Does the sap run freely when the pieces of wood touch?

It would be wonderful to start a relationship with a full fit, but not many of us do, because often at that point in our life we haven't really thought about its importance. Usually that means we have quite a bit of work to do to improve the "fit" or texture of our relationships. It's never too late to change perspectives or improve communication within a relationship; however, the wider the gap the more difficult it is to live together in harmony.

To assess the extent to which there is a natural fit in a relationship, partners or prospective partners can periodically ask themselves the following questions:

1. Do you bring out the best in me?

2. Do I bring out the best in you?

3. Do we bring out the best in each other?

4. Do we have a natural compatibility of values?

5. Are we naturally compatible as people?

6. Do you feel uplifted when you are with me?

7. Do I feel uplifted when I am with you?

8. Do you feel relaxed, free and easy in my presence?

9. Do I feel relaxed, free and easy in your presence?

10. Do I feel loved, valued and respected with you?

11. Do you feel loved, valued and respected with me?

12. Do the circumstances in my life allow me to give my best to you?

13. Do the circumstances in your life allow you to give your best to me?

14. Are we both free enough from bitterness and resentment to give things a chance to really work?

If the answer to most of these questions is *yes*, then there is a natural fit and a great chance of living together in harmony. If the answer to most of these questions is *no*, then there is not a natural fit and it will be a difficult struggle trying to live in harmony. To experience a fulfilling relationship you either have to start with a good fit, change something in the relationship that will allow you to answer most of these questions positively most of the time, or find another relationship with a better fit.

When two people do not "fit," it does not mean that either

is bad. Sometimes they are both great people, but they are not great *together*. Each has good qualities of their own, but they don't bring out each other's best qualities. Sometimes they don't fit because of their backgrounds, life textures, life perspectives or the circumstances in which they live.

To prepare our children and teenagers to enter into meaningful and lasting relationships, we can impress upon them the importance of basic "fit" for long term relationships, and stress the importance of positive communication, mutual respect, celebrating differences, and working and playing together in uplifting ways. We can help them to understand that there are always things to be learned, improved, and nurtured within a relationship, even when the fit is fairly snug at the beginning.

We can help our children become practiced at listening well, expressing their feelings and voicing their concerns, love and compassion. We can teach them the importance of persisting in the face of obstacles and help them learn to cope effectively with stress. This will give them the greatest chance of surviving as individuals and maintaining the quality of ongoing, meaningful relationships. A positive relationship should free us to grow as a person within the relationship and greatly enhance our life. This is a legitimate and worthy quest for our children and ourselves.

Time Together as a Family

Family harmony is largely dependent upon doing cooperative and enjoyable things together as a family, and demonstrating respect for each other's feelings and needs. A harmonious family is very much like a solid sports team. Every player is a valued team member, has an important contribution to make, and knows it. A positive sense of self-worth is generated by including each family member in a meaningful way and by respecting their feelings and input.

Together with your family, identify some uplifting things you can do with each other, or for each other, that will lead to feelings of mutual inclusion, positive interaction and enjoyment. This may include family outings, outdoor excursions, playing cooperative games, simple activities that are fun, special events, family traditions or any activity that ties all family members together in a cooperative way. Cooperative activities, along with clearly identifying positive ways of interacting, will strengthen family bonds and provide an opportunity for parents to share some "good energy" together with the family.

To identify preferred positive activities and positive ways of interacting, ask each family member to share, write or draw their conclusions to the following statements:

1. *It makes me feel good when I . . .*
What are some of your favorite things to do, things that make you feel really good or happy?

2. *It makes me feel good when my family members . . .*
What are some things that the other members of your family do or say that make you feel good? (Answer separately for mom, dad, brother(s), sister(s), dog, cat, etc.)

3. *It makes me feel bad when my family members . . .*
What are some things that the other members of your family do or say that make you feel bad? (Answer separately for mom, dad, brother(s), sister(s), pets, etc.)

4. *It makes others in my family feel good when I . . .*
What are some things *you* can say or do to make each family member feel good? (Answer separately for mom, dad, brother(s), sister(s), pets, etc.)

5. *It makes everybody in my family feel good when we . . .*
What are some things we can all do together as a family that will make us all feel good?

Mealtimes provide an excellent opportunity to develop a sense of togetherness, particularly when family members eat together in a relaxed atmosphere. This is a good time to ask each family member to share the best part of their day (magic moments), to encourage input on various questions or issues, to engage in free and open discussion, and to enjoy an element of humor.

Making the best of time spent together as a family unit is particularly important for large or extended families because one-on-one time with each person may be difficult to achieve. This is also true among team-sport athletes. It is interesting that some of our best team-sport coaches manage to find some one-on-one time for each athlete, each day, even on teams with 15 or 20 players. The coach may simply greet each athlete by name, ask how he's doing today, make a positive comment, put an arm around him or give him a pat on the back. It is greatly appreciated. These athletes know that the coach cares about them, and as a result they contribute more and gain more from the team experience. If you do this with each member of your family, even for a brief period of time every day, each will feel important, respected, special, loved and very much part of the most influential team in their life.

For additional activities to promote positive ways of interacting, see the Activities and Resource section at the back of this book.

Time for Your Child to Play With Other Children

Special time with friends is extremely important for a child's development. It gives children an opportunity to learn how to interact with another young person, highlights the importance of sharing, allows for creative interaction and helps children to feel valued outside the family circle. Ensure that your child has ample opportunities for free play with a friend of his or her choosing, whom he likes and with whom he gets along well.

It "lifts" a child to know that she has her own best friend. She has someone outside the family who likes her and chooses to play with her or be with her. That feels very good for a little person and continues to be important through the years. Opportunities for constructive interaction with other children should be made available as early as possible and become increasingly important as children enter pre-school and the subsequent school years.

Children gain immensely from developing close friendships, kindred spirits or soul mates. They benefit from the quality play experiences that are generated, the close bonds that are created and the special childhood memories associated with a very good friend. They also gain from interacting with children of different ages. Since peers can dramatically influence your children's attitudes and behaviors, do your very best to orchestrate situations where they spend lots of time interacting with other children who project positive, uplifting attributes, humanistic values and healthy life perspectives.

Living Your Life in the Time Zones

How do you feel about your current situation with respect to life in each of the five time zones: time for you, one-on-one time with each child, quality time alone with your partner, time with your family unit together, and time for your child to play or interact with other well-adjusted children? Ask each family member for his or her perception of the present situation, and whether he or she feels there is a need for improvement. The following assessment sheets will help you to do this. After everyone has completed their assessment, sit down together and share your views with other family members. A clear recognition of the need for improvement is a critical first step towards positive change. The remaining steps are believing that something can be done to improve things, deciding to do something, setting a plan of action, and then doing it.

Simple Steps for Improving Life:

1. Complete the following self-assessment sheet for life-time zones.

2. Select a time zone that you feel needs improvement.

3. Set a realistic goal for improvement within that time zone for the upcoming week. Continue to set weekly goals until you are satisfied with life in that zone.

4. When you feel one time zone has reached an acceptable level, if necessary set a goal for improvement in another zone.

5. Take it one step at a time, applauding any progress along the way.

Life-time Zones for Parents

In the spaces provided below, comment on how much quality time you are currently spending in each of the life-time zones, and whether you feel any areas need improvement. For an example of a completed parents' sheet, see the following page.

Life-time Zones	Comment on Your Present Situation	Rate and comment on the need for improvement (use a rating from 0-10, where 0 = no need for improvement and 10 = critical need to improve).
Time for Me (personal space)	_____ _____ _____ _____	_____ _____ _____ _____
One-On-One Time With Each Child	_____ _____ _____ _____	_____ _____ _____ _____
Quality Time Alone With Partner	_____ _____ _____ _____	_____ _____ _____ _____
Time for Family Unit Together	_____ _____ _____ _____	_____ _____ _____ _____
Time for Child to Play or Interact With Other Well-Adjusted Children	_____ _____ _____ _____	_____ _____ _____ _____

In the example provided below, a parent commented on how much quality time she was currently spending in each of the life-time zones, and on which areas she felt were in need of improvement.

Life-time Zones	Comment on Your Present Situation	Rate and comment on the need for improvement (use a rating from 0-10, where 0 = no need for improvement and 10 = critical need to improve).
Time for Me (personal space)	*Generally good.*	*Need for improvement around 3 because there are still portions of days where I feel the need for more personal space.*
One-On-One Time With Each Child	*Shared time with child is great. I've really made a point of making this a priority.*	*Need for improvement around a 2 because there are still times that I would prefer to spend more quality time with just one child.*
Quality Time Alone With Partner	*Shared positive time with partner is far too rare.*	*Need for improvement 8 or 9 if our relationship is to grow.*
Time for Family Unit Together	*Shared time with family is generally very good.*	*I don't see any real need for improvement here although it might be nice to do more as a family every now and then. Around a 1.*
Time for Child to Play or Interact With Other Well-Adjusted Children	*Shared time with other children is generally good. She spends four half days a week playing with a cousin who is very easy going, and goes to a cooperative pre-school two half days a week.*	*No real need for improvement here except perhaps finding another good friend for her to play with more often, rather than always the same person.*

Life-time Zones for Children

Pick a quiet time to sit down with your child to ask him or her the following questions. Bedtime provides a good opportunity for this kind of interaction. Listen closely to the responses without making any judgements, and thank your child for sharing his or her feelings. For an example of one child's responses to these questions see the following page.

Life-time Zones	Child's Comments on Present Situation
Time for you—Do you think you have enough time to play on your own or do things on your own? What do you like to do best playing or doing things on your own?	
Time With Mom—Do you think you have enough special time with just you and Mom? What do you like to do best with Mom?	
Time With Dad—Do you think you have enough special time with just you and Dad? What do you like to do best with Dad?	
Time With Family—Do you think you have enough special time with the whole family together, Mom, Dad, other kids, dog, etc.? What do you like to do best with the whole family?	
Time With a Friend—Do you think you have enough special time playing or doing things with a good friend (or friends)? If no, what would make it better? What things do you like to do best with your friend(s)?	

Life-time Zones	Child's Comments on Present Situation
Time for you—Do you think you have enough time to play on your own or do things on your own? What do you like to do best playing or doing things on your own?	Yah. I like playing with my dolls, playing Lego and playing eat fresh food market (a game she made up herself).
Time With Mom—Do you think you have enough special time with just you and Mom? What do you like to do best with Mom?	Yah. Make little sculptures in clay and going to the farm.
Time With Dad—Do you think you have enough special time with just you and Dad? What do you like to do best with Dad?	Yah. I like to take walks together. I like to play outside together and when you take the time to teach me tricks, and hugging, and another special time is when you read me bedtime stories at night.
Time With Family—Do you think you have enough special time with the whole family together, Mom, Dad, other kids, dog, etc.? What do you like to do best with the whole family?	Not that much because we don't see grandma and grandpa and my aunties and their kids enough, especially the kids. I like it best when everybody comes to dinner at grandma's and we go swimming together.
Time With a Friend—Do you think you have enough special time playing or doing things with a good friend (or friends)? If no, what would make it better? What things do you like to do best with your friend(s)?	No. I'd like more time playing with Emma and Chelsea. I like to play dress-up and fresh food market with them, and eat chocolate chip cookie batter.

Part II

Opening the Door to Human Potential

It's a mystery how the very best people are always open and receptive to learning, while the worst already know everything.

The Challenge of Parenting

Learn to listen like a Teddy Bear,
With ears open and mouth closed tight
Learn to forgive like a Teddy Bear,
With heart open, not caring who is right
Learn to love like a Teddy Bear,
With arms open and imperfect eyesight.

— *Sarah McClellan*

Parenting is the most important job in the world. Nowhere else is your influence so directly felt, or your existence so important to the development of another human being. This is why each of us must do everything in our power to become the best parents we can possibly be. The quest for excellence in parenting is challenging and sometimes frustrating, yet it brings with it some of life's greatest rewards.

The guiding light for quality parenting was communicated to me simply and eloquently by my five-year-old daughter. One morning after I had been playing with her group of pre-school children she skipped over to me, looked at me wide-eyed and said, "I really like you—'cause you're nice on my feelings." Then she sauntered off. That was a magic moment.

On another occasion a mother was dragging her child along by the arm, down a city street. The child pleaded with his Mom to stop for a moment so he could play. When she refused, his request turned to despair and he uttered, "Mommy you broke my feelings".

To grow towards their true potential and flourish as

human beings, children need someone in their life who believes in them, who accepts them totally, who loves them without placing conditions on that love, who is nice on their feelings. It's not, "I'll love you if you do this or if you don't do that; it's simply "I love you." People who excel at living have had one such person in their life—a mother, father, grandparent, teacher, coach . . . someone. Who will that person be in your child's life?

Children at all ages are bright and responsive little people with high needs for love and acceptance. Very small children have very big and sensitive feelings, and they are tremendously affected by our response or lack of response to their feelings. When children cry out for our love or contact and no one responds, they feel abandoned, rejected and very much alone. This is very hurtful on their feelings of self-worth. It makes them feel unworthy, incompetent and less valued as people.

If we were simply nicer on children's feelings, they would take a giant leap forward in terms of their total human development. "Nice on a child's feelings" implies that we respect the child as a sensitive and fully feeling human being, at any age and stage. It means that we stop and think about a child's feelings *before* rather than after we act or react. Every time we are positive, loving and supportive with our children, other people and with nature, we nourish the genuine humanity which is alive within all children—all around the world. Every time we hurt a child's feelings we chip away at their spontaneity, self-respect and love for life.

Children's early judgements about their own value, capabilities and worth are based primarily on how they are treated and nurtured by important people around them. There are so many good reasons to give time, love and high-quality care during these early years. You will never again have the opportunity to be so important, or so close, to another human being. And you will probably never grow as much yourself, as you will by taking full advantage of this opportunity.

Cherish This Time

Your child's birth was a magical moment. Through you a totally unique and special little person entered this world. You have been presented with a wonderful opportunity but also an enormous responsibility. For the first time in your life another human being is totally dependent upon you for survival.

As a new parent, your life is altered in some very significant ways. You come to know the true meaning of giving, totally giving of yourself for another's benefit, and you struggle with how to share your love and life without choking off your own needs for growth and space. You experience an incredible bond with a tiny human being—a bond closer and stronger than you ever imagined possible.

I have often wondered how we can get so close to little children, so quickly, and why this relationship feels so meaningful and complete. I think one reason is because of children's open-armed love and acceptance of us, as we are. The other reason is because they need us, and we feel that need. Some of us have never before felt so needed or so loved.

Take full advantage of the magic moments afforded to you by this opportunity. Cherish your child's open-armed, totally absorbing hugs, where he wraps his little arms and legs around you and snuggles into you like a little bear cub. Soak in the magic moments where he abandons himself to you and frees you to feel totally connected, needed, wanted, appreciated, loved and loving in the tenderest of ways. The human bond felt during these moments can be more complete and deeper than anything you have previously experienced.

Open yourself to your child's playful explorations and her many "special" discoveries. In the early years almost everything that she sees, hears, touches, tastes, smells, learns or discovers is magic. Each new discovery brings joy, excitement and wonder, whether it be learning to roll over, walk, make a sound, talk, open cupboards, touch a worm, watch a bird, explore a flower, dress herself, draw, question, blow a bubble, ride a bicycle alone, take a stroke in the water, swim, jump, dive or whistle. Almost every day there are "firsts" that you can share and enjoy together if you spend time with your child and remain attentive when you do.

By "living" these magic moments with your children, you are rewarded for the frustrations, and you find joy in days that may otherwise seem to drag on forever. Enjoy the magic moments you have together. This special time of childhood passes quickly and is gone forever.

On my daughter's fifth birthday it seemed like only yesterday, and yet a lifetime ago, that she was born. When she first started school I felt apprehensive, but also extremely fortunate that I had taken the time to really enjoy being with her during those previous five years. It had been the most special time of my life. I felt that I had shared my greatest influence, for better or worse, because I knew that now the outside world would come in more and more—school, peers, older children, teachers, other adults, television, movies, books, various subcultures—and each have its impact. Our children are always our children, yet as they grow older you cannot carve the wind and waves that now begin to shape their destiny as much as you once did.

In the ensuing years I realized that watching a child grow into a stronger and more self-sufficient person is a wonderful process to be a part of. Each step represents a new era in their development, and your development. They may have less time for you, but the shorter times you have together can be rich and meaningful. You do not have to become less of a parent, even though you are now an active parent for less of the time. When your children know in their hearts that you will always be there for them, your relationship continues to grow in enriching and impactful ways for a long time, even after they have their own children.

I have cherished the many special moments afforded to me by the children in my life, and have grown immensely from those experiences. I have learned to live a higher quality of life, to balance my work and play, and to recognize the true essence of living each magic moment. I am much wiser and more complete as a person because of what I have learned from children. They have taught me well.

Expressions Of Love

The biggest deficit in the world today
is the deficit of attention
for children
from parents.

Above all, express your love today and every day.
Make sure your children know that their presence is treasured
and their feelings really count.
This is the path to confidence, gentle strength
and fulfillment within children.

The path to self-confidence, stability and emotional strength within children lies in expressions of love.

Who made you feel most loved, appreciated, accepted, respected and valued when you were a child? What did they do that made you feel valued and loved?

The potential sources of love are many—parents, grandparents, friends, friends' parents, sisters, brothers, relatives, caregivers, teachers, coaches, teammates, even pets. They make you feel loved and special by showing their affection, sharing their time, listening attentively, projecting belief in you, providing support and creating special memories of caring. The following quotations from teenagers and young adults, provide real examples of things parents have done to make their children feel loved, appreciated and emotionally secure in life.

Show Your Affection

- *Mom frequently told me that she loved me. She would often say that if she could be young again she'd want to be just like me.*

- *Dad accepted me as I was and didn't put me down for being me. He showed me that I was wanted, that he was happy I was his child.*

- *Mom showed lots of physical affection—hugs, hugs and more hugs. She told me she loved me and that she would love me no matter what.*

- *When Dad gave me a big hug and said "I love you" it made me feel so good inside. It still does.*

- *I wish my parents would have told me that they loved me. I can't remember them saying it even once. Even as a child I remember feeling insecure. I'm sure that if I had been reassured of their love, it would have helped a lot.*

Share Your Time

- *Mom made me feel as if I was the most important person to her, talking, sharing time together, even doing nothing together.*

- *When I was younger, Mom took the time to play with me, talk with me, listen to me, help me with homework, and help me out with problems. Those earlier years set the basis for our super relationship now. I still go home whenever I can because I enjoy being there.*

- *My parents always took me places. I felt as though they wanted me around and didn't want to escape from me.*

- *My Dad took the time to be with me, play with me, talk to me, go for a walk with me, which made me feel happy and* important. I knew he really cared about me because he showed an interest in my activities and spent one-on-one time with me.

- I wish my parents had taken more time to be with me. When they don't spend time with you it's hard to believe that they really care.

Listen Attentively

- From an early age my parents treated me as an individual and asked me how I felt about things. They really listened to me, like I was the most important person in the world. It made me feel that I mattered even as a little person.

- Mom always seemed to be there to listen to what I had to say. When I came home from school she was very interested in what I did, who I played with, and how I was feeling. When I was depressed or feeling sad, she always seemed to be able to find something positive in those situations.

- Mom and Dad have always made us feel that our opinions were important from the time we could talk. I remember as a little girl sitting at the dinner table with my dad and his sister. I made a comment about the situation being discussed and my aunt totally ignored it and rudely cut me off. My Dad piped up and said, "Hey Marg, Anne has something to say and you might just learn something from her." Did I feel respected!

- We were always included in the family plans (vacations, out-ings, activities). Our input was considered important. I was encouraged to express my feelings. I felt important, accepted and wanted whenever they listened to me. It made me feel understood, loved and accepted.

- My parents never expressed their love verbally or physically *and they never took the time to listen to me. I was starved for attention and ended up being a terrible kid. I used to fight, steal and do anything to get attention. Only now have I begun to understand that my parents probably cared for all their children but never showed it. I wish they had.*

Project Your Belief

- *My parents gave me a lot of confidence by often reminding me of my strengths, and they often commented on my strengths to others when I was able to hear. When they complimented me or told someone else about something good I had done, it made me feel appreciated and really happy.*

- *Mom always told me I could do anything I wanted to do. She always believed in me, no matter how I did. That gave me self-confidence. It created a feeling of belief in myself.*

- *In all the situations where I felt loved and wanted, I always felt respected. That respect really makes you feel like a somebody. Mom was always respectful of decisions I made, which made me feel great. She allowed me to make my own decisions. She encouraged me to be adventurous and challenged me to pursue my dreams, however far-fetched they might have seemed. She instilled a belief in me that I could do anything.*

- *My Dad provided unconditional love and encouragement. That made me believe in myself, my qualities, my thinking.*

- *My parents did nothing outstanding or memorable that made me feel respected, loved or special. If I look back to when I got beaten as a child, I hated my parents then. Now I think maybe they cared about me but I wish they were less strict and more able to show me I was loved in my early years.*

Provide Support

- *Dad always praised effort in any endeavor, large or small, and downplayed results. He never yelled at me, he always explained the why behind doing something or not doing something. He made me feel good about being the way I am.*

- *With Mom there was a lot of shared laughing, lots of physical and verbal support and she smiled at the right moment — when I needed it. She used to tell me that I helped her a lot — even when I was little. Those were always proud and happy moments.*

- *Mom understood my fears and was always there for me. She accepted me in all my moods and was patient with me. That helped me a lot. The biggest and most important thing I felt from my parents was a genuine concern for my well-being. That was the greatest gift.*

- *Things that are important to me became important to them. They would sacrifice something they wanted to do for something I wanted to do.*

- *Unfortunately, I cannot recall my parents doing a single thing that made me feel accepted or loved. They were a money oriented couple — their life revolved around it. I needed love as a child more than anything, and I didn't get it. The family functioned more as an institutional unit of which I was a member. I was always competing and fighting for recognition. I never got it from them. I sought this affection and recognition from friends. They became the veins and arteries in my body that led to my survival. That initial lack of love and support from my parents led to some real insecurities within me and to some serious ongoing emotional problems in my brothers and sister.*

Create Special Memories of Caring

- *Dad used to take me out for lunch once a week—just me by myself. He still does. It's our special time together.*

- *My Mom had homemade bread, tarts, or cookies waiting for me when I arrived home. I think this is when I felt the most loved and wanted. I also felt special when my mom made something special for dinner—everyone was there but it was my favorite.*

- *My Mom would write little notes in my lunch box. That was special, and when it rained or was too cold, my dad would take me around in the car to deliver on my paper route.*

- *Dad and I used to take our dog for walks in the parks outside the city. That was a special time for us because it was something that just the two of us did together.*

- *Sitting close, snuggling and reading stories to me at night was always a special time. When I was five years old I remember feeling loved by my parents when the whole family (six kids) was together at the cottage drinking hot chocolate around the woodstove on a cold night. There was a special feeling of warmth and Mom and Dad seemed really "into" us. There was attention for all and everyone got along well.*

Children recognize true value within themselves when they feel "valued" by people who are important to them. This begins at an early age. Children grow to believe in themselves, and their own capacity, when they are treated in ways that make them feel valued, competent and loved. When they feel inadequate, insecure or unhappy with themselves it is often because they feel that the people they value most, are unhappy with them. They end up feeling that they always fall short of the expectations that others have for them. If they are not given time, attention, love or respect, most will conclude, "My parents are not really interested in me, my activities, my feelings or my opinions—therefore I must not be a very good or worthwhile person." Parents may view the issue as revolving around a lack of time. Children view it as a lack of interest— "You must not be interested enough in me or like me enough to choose to spend time with me or to treat me with respect." Early challenges to self-acceptance and self-confidence can leave children feeling fragile for a very long time.

Being "Nice on My Feelings"

The guiding light for strong and self-confident children lives within our capacity to be respectful of feelings, our own feelings and our children's feelings. When we are respectful, sensitive and caring for feelings, we enrich the lives of others as well as our own lives. When we are disrespectful, insensitive or uncaring of feelings, we shatter dreams, threaten confidence, destroy relationships and dampen the spark that gives essence to life.

Being nice on children's feelings is the best way to inflate little balloons of hope, self-respect, joy and self-confidence within them. Imagine for a moment that your child is made up of a collection of brightly colored little balloons. Every positive experience or interaction you have with your child inflates a tiny balloon of light, deep within your child. This allows your child to blossom with a sense of security, confidence, self-esteem, warmth, happiness and belief in his or her own capacity. The better you and others become at inflating balloons that are uplifting to children, the stronger and more resilient they grow to be.

It is inevitable that some balloons will be popped along the way, but if you start by inflating many balloons with positive experiences, your child will gain enough inner strength to remain strong even in the face of adversity. With continued support your child will eventually learn to inflate or reinflate his or her own balloons.

People's lives rest in a delicate balance between personal balloons inflated and popped, most often by those closest to them. By inflating—and not deflating—little balloons, you create a special sense of respect and meaningfulness within your children, your relationships and yourself.

I remember getting up early one Sunday morning, going into the kitchen and, together with my young daughter, making some special crepes for breakfast. We poured in the flour, milk and eggs, and she began to mix it all together very diligently. Just as the mixture was starting to look great she tipped the bowl over. It oozed out onto the counter, the floor and onto her feet. As I grabbed for a cloth I said, "No problem, Anouk, we've still got lots left in our bowl for our crepes, and you did a great job mixing it. I've tipped stuff over before. We're lucky that we've got lots left." I wiped off the counter and her feet, as she swirled interesting designs into the remaining mixture on the floor. I thanked her for helping me clean up and for doing such a good mixing job. She smiled, walked over to me and gave me the biggest hug—which we held for a long time. She said, "I like it when if I spill something by accident, like crepes or milk, or break a plate, you don't get mad at me, 'cause lots of parents get mad at their kids and yell. You always say the good parts about me spilling it and not the bad parts. They always tell the bad parts or what kids did wrong. It's better to make them feel better and not feel worse, 'cause they already feel worse."

The problem with getting mad, yelling or chastising children for not being more perfect or more adult is that it's not very nice on their feelings and you are essentially telling them they are not OK the way they are. The fact is they are children—not adults. Children drop things, knock things over, they don't like sitting quietly, they're not very tidy, they don't remember where they put things, they stop to absorb themselves in the present and don't relate well to the concept of being on our time. Should we make them feel "bad," unworthy, incompetent or inadequate as people, simply for being what they are at this stage of their development? Do we really want them to be adults when they are four or five years old? They will be adults soon enough—forever.

All of us are sometimes guilty of making comments or

doing things that are less than best for our children's self-esteem. We do this without any malicious intent and sometimes are not even aware that we are doing it. For example, one child brought out a beautiful collection of pencils to show me. She was very proud of her collection and told me that after she had taken her collection of pencils to school, all of her friends started to collect pencils too. One of her parents who had overheard our conversation piped in at that point and said, "Well, they're not collecting pencils because of you—it's just a fad now." The little girl lowered her head, sank into her chair and made no comment. I felt her little balloon of pride break inside her. Her momentary sense of importance melted away. I moved closer to her, touched her on the shoulder and quietly said, "I think those kids started to collect pencils because of you; I've seen it happen with other things before." She commented, "Well, at least somebody believes me."

Her parent was a good person, never beat her child, wasn't yelling at her, but she broke a little balloon, unnecessarily.

On another outing a woman with a five-year-old boy was sitting next to me at an ice skating show. Many children in the audience had sparkling lights which glowed as they waved them in the darkened arena. Her son was excited about being out with his mom and about her buying him this sparkling light. He was waving this thing around just like all the other kids. It must have been distracting for his mother because she grabbed it out of his hand, stuffed it inside her coat and sternly told him to sit still and watch the performance. He was having a great time doing his own performance with his little flashlight until she popped his balloon. The boy sat quietly. Much of his joy and excitement had withered away. He was no longer in control and no longer felt so special or loved.

Another evening a group of children went out together to skate on a large outdoor rink and see some ice sculptures. They stopped at a concession stand for a treat. One parent who was there as a volunteer helper refused to allow her daughter to have a treat, even after her daughter pleaded the

familiar plea, "But all the other kids are having one." The parent's rationale was that her daughter had already eaten a
cookie earlier that day. The girl who had been so excited about
her mother coming on the outing with her, ended up feeling
unhappy, resentful, unloved and wishing that her mother had
not come. Good nutrition is extremely important, and we
should try to provide the healthiest foods possible. However,
there are times when nutrition for the body must give way to
nutrition for the mind, and for strengthening a relationship.
This was one such time.

Breaking a few balloons is not going to result in a major
disaster. However, if over a number of months or years, parents, caregivers, teachers or coaches get in a habit of popping
little balloons by subjecting children to negative experiences or
negative comments, one by one children begin to sag, deflate
and shrivel up inside. If enough balloons are broken the child
will end up with very low self-esteem, often feeling that he
can't do *anything* right. Although you may love him dearly
and believe in his capacity, he may still feel inadequate, insecure, rejected or resentful as a result of these broken balloons.
Worst of all he may begin to see himself as unworthy of love
and useless as a person.

Why put children's emotional health at risk by breaking
little balloons, when you can just as easily inflate them? Stop
and think about how you can inflate more balloons or be nicer
on your children's feelings. Remind yourself to act in positive
ways *before* you enter situations where you will interact with
children.

The Way of Saving Face

I have discovered a respectful and effective way of communicating with children that guards their sense of dignity and self-
worth. I call it the way of saving face. It allows you to nurture
a child's growth while preserving the child's honor, confidence
and self-esteem. It is an attempt to teach with respect instead

of relying on showdowns, power struggles or force.

Lots of conflicts arise because we attempt to directly control children instead of giving them some responsibility or sense of control over their own choices. Conflicts often arise over seemingly insignificant things, such as choice of clothes, coats, boots, mitts, etc. We gain nothing by fighting or arguing about choices on the way out the door ("You shouldn't have worn those boots; you should have worn the other coat"); all we end up doing is getting ourselves upset and making the child feel inadequate, unloved or angry.

Let's say your child selects a coat to wear which you feel is inappropriate, perhaps because you feel it may not be warm enough. Instead of saying, you can't wear that or that's a stupid choice, you could say, "That coat looks good on you—I just hope it's warm enough. Let's bring an extra one which is warmer just in case." In this case no damage is done to the child's self-esteem, her capacity to choose is respected, a lesson is communicated about warmth and you have a warmer coat with you just in case. If it is really cold outside the child will want to put on the warmer coat.

Another respectful option which helps children learn to make good choices is to say, "Go outside for a few minutes and see how cold it is—then decide which jacket you think you need." The emphasis here is on respectful long-term learning.

There is another way of saving face I often use when I feel something is important, but the child is not mentally prepared or ready to accept my suggestion at that moment. I call it the "next time" approach, and it is aimed at saving face and promoting long-term learning. Let me illustrate this approach with a few examples.

I bought my daughter a bicycle helmet when she was five or six years old. Before we went for our first bike ride that year, I took out her new helmet and tried to get her to wear it. She wasn't overjoyed with the helmet idea. For her it felt heavy and made her head look big and funny. She did not want to wear it. I explained to her that it was the best helmet for protecting her head and brain, and that was the important thing. And the bike racers wear them too! She still resisted. I chose to not force a showdown on the issue at that moment (for example, by saying, "Wear it or we're not going") because I knew it would end up with her crying, me upset and an afternoon spoiled. I also felt that if she had time to think about the helmet she would choose to wear it for good reasons. So I said, "OK, today we'll go for a short ride on a closed-off road where there are no cars or people, without the helmet, and you can wear your helmet *next time*." This saved face for her, made our day enjoyable and gave her time to mentally prepare herself to wear the helmet next time.

The next time we were preparing to go for a bike ride I put my helmet on and said nothing about her helmet, which was hanging next to her bike. She picked it up, put it on and repeated to me what I had said to her the day before. "It's good for protecting your head and it doesn't really matter what it looks like." The important information had settled in without force, and she was now freer to make a good choice.

As you begin to use the "next time" approach with your children, they will begin to use it back with you. Here are some real examples:

Child: *The lunch was good, but next time could you please cut the sandwich in two?*

Parent: *Sure. Thanks for telling me so I know what you would prefer for next time.*

Child: *I don't want to hurt your feelings, but next time could you let me choose what I want to drink?*

Parent: *Sorry, I didn't realize I did that. I'll make sure I do it for next time. Thanks for telling what you were feeling.*

Child: *Dad, the chocolate milk is OK, but it's pretty strong. Maybe next time you can add a little less cocoa.*

Parent: *Would you like me to make you another glass?*

Child: *No, no it's fine. It's just for next time.*
(Smiles all around the table.)

Child: *Ouch, that's my sore ear.* (Parent accidentally touched her daughter's sore ear while putting her to bed.)
Parent: *Sorry, I forgot.*
Child: *It's OK, it's just for next time.*
Parent: *I like it when you tell me about next time like that. You remind me of what to do next time without making me feel bad.*
(Child smiles, rolls over and drifts off to sleep.)

The "next time" approach makes children feel good about themselves, and it also makes you feel good when you are on the receiving end. Neither parent nor child is expected to instantly change things that cannot be immediately changed or to alter things that have already happened. Both parent and child are free to learn a lesson for next time, and the whole learning process is very respectful of people and their feelings.

Important lessons can be drawn out and communicated respectfully even in situations where children have behaved carelessly, dangerously or in a manner which has not respected the feelings of others. In essence you tell the child, "I love you. I respect you. I know you didn't try to do anything wrong, but there is an important lesson here which can help for next time." The child continues to feel valued while learning the lesson.

When children grow with respect, it is natural for them to treat others with respect. They learn about communication, expressing feelings, making good choices and assuming responsibility often by the example you provide. When children are free to learn with love, respect and a sense of personal worth, and are also expected to draw out lessons from their experiences, things remain positive and never seem to get blown out of proportion.

Nurturing Cooperation and Empathy

Positive early experiences with cooperation and sharing, free children to play joyfully, love completely, live and work in harmony and compete in a healthy way.

When you share your time and love with children, it is the most natural thing in the world for them to want to share something in return. By sharing with you, *they* feel important, gain a sense of personal control and experience joy from including you in their discoveries. Young children love to share their "finds," "treasures" and new discoveries, and the more responsive you are to this kind of sharing, the more it will occur.

Gestures of sharing and giving surface early and often in a child's life. You simply have to tune into these gestures and applaud them to help cooperation grow. Very young children may offer a drink from their bottle, a taste of mushed food, a teddy bear, toy, bug or hug. If you reach out and gratefully accept their many "gifts," you nurture their natural inclination towards sharing. Accept, admire and enjoy their offerings and gratefully return them. Play a little game of "give and give," where they give and you return, and you give and they return, whether it be with hugs, teddy bears or an old sock. If you fail to accept their offerings, you can unwittingly cut off these sharing gestures before they have had a chance to fully develop.

From my work with pre-school and kindergarten children it is clear that those who are liked best by their peers are those who are most skilled at cooperation and sharing. Children who have learned to share are readily included in play activities and most desired as friends. Teachers also enjoy being with these children.

The least liked children are those who are most aggressive and who have not developed skills for cooperation or sharing. The reason these children are not liked and not chosen as play-mates is because they hit, push, shove, grab everything for themselves, try to boss everyone around, take things from other children, without giving anything in return, and lie (for example, say they didn't have a turn or a candy when they already had more turns or candies than anyone else). These children have not yet developed effective skills for interacting with their peers in a cooperative or empathetic way.

The early nurturing of skills for cooperation and sharing is important not only for living in harmony, but also because your child's early acceptance by peers is largely dependent upon it. Acceptance or rejection from other children, even at age four or five, has a strong influence on your child's emerging self-confidence, self-acceptance and feelings of self-worth.

Children who do not acquire sharing skills in their early years, frequently do not understand why no one wants to play with them. Occasionally I have taken one of these children aside and tried to explain in the gentlest way I can that people do not like other people when they just take things and never share what they have. I tell them, "If you change the way you treat other children, they will change the way they treat you." The simple fact is that neither children nor adults like it when someone acts in totally non-sharing or destructive ways.

For children to become skilled at cooperation and sharing they need opportunities to practice interacting with other children in constructive ways. The earlier this begins the better. In the early years you can guide some of this interaction in a positive direction by helping them learn to share simple play-things. For example, with one and two year olds you can sit them down facing each other with legs apart and direct them through a simple game of rolling a ball back and forth. Guide the exchange a number of times, being sure you tell them how great they are doing. Then step back. They will likely continue to enjoy the process on their own.

If there is a conflict between two children over a single toy, make an effort to show them how they can both have fun together by sharing the same toys. For example, if two children are tugging on the same scooter or wagon, put them both on the scooter and "wheel" them around the room. Give each of them a turn up front in the driver's seat. Then step back. They will often figure out a way to move themselves around together, either by both pushing together on the floor with their feet, or by taking turns.

Children develop an early history of sharing if they are given opportunities to play with others in a nurturing environment that fosters humanistic values. By age three or four, most children nurtured through cooperative activities share and help one another with some regularity. Cooperative skills learned in play are readily integrated into living. Through cooperative playful experiences, children can become immersed in something joyous and at the same time extract valuable lessons for living.

I have created a series of activities specifically designed to help children develop their cooperative skills through play and games. They are called Cooperative Games. [See *The Cooperative Sports & Games Book* listed with other resources at the back of this book.] The distinctive feature of these games lies in their design and the way in which they are played. For example, in the cooperative game "Children on the Mountain," the goal is for the children to help as many of their friends as possible get to the top of "the mountain." Children play together to accomplish this goal. This frees them from the pressure to compete, eliminates the need for destructive behavior and encourages helpful and fun-filled interaction.

The concept is simple. Children are encouraged to play *with* one another rather than *against* one another, to overcome challenges rather than overcome other people and to enjoy the playful experience itself.

The major goal of cooperative play and games is to enable children to become more receptive to, and skilled at, cooperation and sharing. Ultimately this will lead to sharing ideas, talents, concerns, feelings, respect, possessions, equipment, turns, time, space, responsibility—and the betterment of each other's lives.

Genuine cooperation is choosing to cooperate because you care about others, truly want to help them or enjoy interacting with them in positive ways, rather than cooperating to gain some personal advantage for yourself. True cooperation is a positive attitude or value, and not a strategy for personal gain.

A positive orientation towards cooperation and sharing is not something that can be transmitted in a few minutes. It takes lots of encouragement and persistence on your part, as well as setting a positive example to follow. It is well worth the effort.

Nurturing Empathy

Knowing may be important, but it is feeling that takes us to a higher level of humanity.

Cooperation and empathy are very closely linked. Together they are the most important skills affecting positive human interaction and human survival. The degree to which a person is capable of empathizing with others is the best barometer of how that person will treat and respond to others throughout his or her life. The value of acquiring skills that allow us to empathize and communicate respectfully with others is increasingly apparent as our society becomes progressively more competitive, technical and violent in make-up. Empathy is the only true antidote for violence, destructiveness and the breakdown of human relationships.

If we raise the level of empathy among people in the world, the world will ultimately become a much safer, more humane and joyful place to live. Empathy creates the foundation for love, compassion, harmony, respect, true cooperation and higher levels of humanity.

Empathy is totally grounded in feelings—*experiencing* feelings, *acknowledging* feelings, *sharing* feelings, *"reading"* feelings, *understanding* and *respecting* feelings, and most important, *feeling others' feelings*.

Without empathy there is no true humanity, no genuine cooperation and no chance of human relationships flourishing into what they can be. You need only watch "the news" to witness the frightening horrors inflicted on fellow human beings, daily. The perpetrators of these horrendous acts have one thing in common. They have no empathy. They have no feelings, or caring for, the feelings of others. Only when there is an absence of empathy is it possible to commit such degrading acts. If you look closely at people who hurt, abuse, put down or destroy others, they are all underdeveloped in the same way. They lack empathy and compassion. They do not feel, or care about, the feelings of others. This absence of empathy is at the root of all destructive acts.

The more empathy a person develops towards others, the more impossible it is for them to knowingly hurt others—physically, psychologically or emotionally. Empathy, more than anything else, immunizes people against being destructive, degrading or violent towards others. You cannot knowingly or intentionally hurt other people when you have genuine empathy for their feelings. To do so would hurt you too much, because you care about their feelings, know how they feel and feel how you would feel in their position.

Empathy is the skill that allows you to *feel* another person's perspective or plight on an emotional level and to really care about what happens to him or her. It is a different skill from being able to know something on an intellectual level. The extent to which this skill is present or absent either liberates or destroys individuals, relationships, families, communities and societies.

Harmonious interaction among adults begins with what we experience as children. Have we learned to really feel what others are feeling? Have we become competent at really feeling and communicating our own feelings? Those who are abusive towards others, who treat others with disrespect or take unfair advantage of them, either never developed these skills as children or lost them somewhere along the way. People who genuinely care about others, who strive for more positive and fulfilling relationships or hope to create a more humane world, are guided by high levels of empathy.

How do we learn empathy? How do we nurture it within our children?

Empathy is best learned in childhood by helping children become connected to their own feelings and to the feelings of others. The most important aspect of nurturing empathy in children is the overall message you communicate about the value of others and the importance of feelings. Children will develop empathy skills at an early age when you express your own inner feelings, show an interest in their feelings, talk about how other people might feel, and ask them how they feel others might feel.

Empathy centers on creating and building upon a natural disposition for caring, connecting, feeling and cooperating. You can begin to nurture empathy within children by talking with them about feelings, by reading stories where characters demonstrate a genuine concern for others, by guiding them to act in considerate ways in their play, by providing them with social toys or toy families, and by encouraging their gentleness with animals and fellow humans. If you provide a positive example to follow, and encourage empathy through their play, children will begin to express and act out their concern for others, even at two or three years of age.

Books and Stories

You can often see the beginnings of empathy when children listen intently to stories. They clearly identify with some of the characters in these stories and become very concerned about their welfare. This is communicated through facial expressions, body movements, sounds of concern and the questions they ask. It is clear that many children feel an emotional connection to storybook characters. During or following stories (or movies), you can seize the moment to help empathy grow. Ask the children to tell you what they were feeling inside themselves during specific parts of the story. Accept their feelings. Ask them how they feel the character in the story was feeling. Share your own feelings as well, so they know how you feel the character might have been feeling. Let them know it's good to feel real human emotions. These feelings tell us we are fully alive, fully human and capable of caring.

For my daughter's second birthday I gave her a "Winnie the Pooh" book. As she thumbed through the book, she stopped at a picture of Winnie the Pooh lying flat on his back with Tigger standing over him. She surveyed the picture, pointed at Pooh and repeatedly said, "OK? OK? OK?" I told her that Tigger had bounced into Pooh by accident but that Pooh was fine, he was OK. That seemed to relieve her concern, and she flipped the page.

Playacting in Considerate Ways

An excellent way to actively promote empathy skills in young children is to encourage them to act out, or play through, various helping scenarios. For example, in one book there is a drawing of a little bird shivering, when he has fallen into the snow. While reading stories like this, you can ask your child to imagine how the little bird feels. Then ask him to make-believe that he is gently picking up the little bird out of the snow, warming him and returning him to his home in the tree. It helps if the children physically and mentally act out these positive steps in their pretend play.

In another story a little raccoon falls into the water and is struggling to climb out. Stop and ask your child how she feels the raccoon might be feeling, as well as what she thinks she could do to help. By imagining what these characters might feel, it helps the child to better understand the feelings and needs of other living beings. "Pretending" that she is helping encourages her to act on feelings of concern for animals or people, large or small. If you initiate this process with two- and three-year-old children they will soon begin to feel, help, comfort and express warm human emotion while listening to stories, watching films and playing, as well as in their own lives outside of play.

Playing With Make-Believe Families

The acting out and refinement of empathy skills can be effectively nurtured by providing children with "toy families" with which they can play. Variously sized versions of the same wooden animals, cuddly teddy bears, dolls or puppets work well to represent family members of different sexes, sizes and ages. Empathy seems to be drawn out more readily with children when they play with babies, so make sure their make-believe families include baby animals and baby people. They seem to easily imagine these babies "needing" them, and this draws out positive responses in the same way real babies draw out empathy from their parents when they perceive a real need.

Providing children with toy families creates many opportunities for engaging their "players" in positive and interactive ways. Through this type of play they can act out positive concerns for animals, dolls, teddy bears and people, by cuddling them, rocking them, talking to them and safely tucking them under the covers for bed at night. You can join in this play and encourage or reinforce your child for acting in positive and responsive ways.

One of the major problems with war toys or warrior-type toys is that it encourages children to play in non-empathetic ways. Warrior toys are used to act out fighting, killing and destroying others. This works contrary to the goal of promoting empathy towards other human beings. When engaging warriors in battle, children rarely play in positive or empathetic ways. They do not direct their charges into positive interaction with families, babies or little people, because all the "players" are warriors and they are in a war zone. Clearly, this is not conducive to the learning or acting out of empathy.

Caring for Animals

Positive contact with animals and pets is a wonderful way to encourage the development of empathy skills in young children. Baby animals are particularly good in this regard, especially if children are given an opportunity to admire them at close range, cuddle them softly, pat them gently or care for them respectfully. Springtime provides a great opportunity to connect with newborn ducks, geese, horses, puppies and fawns.

I once observed a two-year-old child trying to get close enough for intimate interaction with a kitten. She sat on the floor right next to him and observed carefully as he lapped up his milk. She offered him a bottle, nipple first. I'm sure she was thinking that he couldn't possibly refuse that. He turned and walked away. She persisted by offering him crayons, a coloring book, a sleeping box, hugs and finally small pieces of fish. He accepted the latter, and that was the beginning of a great friendship. On other occasions, I have observed children hand-feeding wild birds and bottle-feeding baby goats, calves, baby kangaroos and even wolf cubs. It is always a special experience for the child and creates special bonds of caring.

The birth of any animal provides a unique opportunity for children to experience one of life's most incredible events and to take part in the nurturing that follows. It is a great opportunity to help children develop respect for the rights and needs of other living beings, appreciation of their fragility and an understanding of how to touch with gentleness and care ("as gentle as a feather"). It may take some time for a very young child to be completely respectful with a baby kitten or puppy, but with guidance they do become gentle, protective and nurturing, and they soon begin to "teach" their human visitors to be equally gentle.

Outdoor settings provide another excellent opportunity to develop a genuine sense of empathy and respect for other living things. For example, when children encounter frogs or grasshoppers, or anything living, encourage them to be gentle, to be careful, to not hurt it, to be respectful of its feelings and its life, to look closely and then to return it to where they found it, unharmed. Remind them that animals in the wild have homes, families and friends and a right to live, just as we do.

Good films about animals in their natural environment can also help to communicate a caring perspective. When my daughter was five years old we watched a program about Jane Goodall's work with wild chimpanzees. In this documentary, some of the chimpanzees got sick, and Jane discovered the mother of a five-year-old chimp named Flo, lying dead next to a stream. At this point my daughter snuggled into my side, leaned her head on my shoulder and began to cry. Clearly she could empathize with that little five-year-old chimp, Flo, who lost her mother. When the film finished, we went outside for a walk. As we walked along, we talked and exchanged feelings about life and death and getting old and dying.

This kind of sharing is an important part of becoming fully human. It is largely through developing skills for empathy that we learn to really feel things, to care about others, to understand and accept the feelings of others, to act in humane and respectful ways and to experience life fully.

TV and Empathy

One of the obstacles we face in nurturing positive and empathetic children is that they get contrary messages from other mediums. They are entertained with violence. They are exposed to countless cartoon characters and violent heroes who hit, punch, flatten, shoot, and resolve conflicts in abusive ways. This constant negative programming that occurs through these mediums serves to decrease empathy and increase aggression. The effects are obvious in children's play, in our schools and in increased levels of abuse in the home and on the street. *We cannot entertain children and youth with violence, and not entertain heightened levels of violence in our society and in our lives.*

One of the major problems with the extensive viewing of violence in movies and on TV is that it destroys or weakens empathy. It numbs people's feelings about others, which in turn makes them less caring and more capable of destructive acts. After witnessing thousands of TV incidents depicting aggression, insensitivity, violence with no remorse, even joy in killing, it is easier to lash out at others or to ignore the feelings of people in need, without *feeling* anything at all.

Negative programming against empathy, cooperation and respect for the true values of life, makes our job as parents and teachers much more difficult, because we are pulling in one direction and these other forces are pulling in another. But it doesn't make our job impossible, because some children in living our culture grow into wonderful, humanistic adults.

The job of nurturing children in positive directions is greatly facilitated when children are exposed to positive role models both on television and in their immediate environment. Our children need and gain immensely from gentle heroes who portray positive ways of living and respectful ways of resolving conflicts. If responsible parents who work in the television, film and video-game industry would consider the serious implications of the models they provide for millions of children, we would take a huge step forward in humanizing our world. These mediums have a tremendous capacity to enrich or destroy empathy and cooperative values within children. Why not use these mediums in positive ways to enrich life rather than destroy it?

The options we have as parents are 1) to eliminate TV and video equipment from our homes, 2) to restrict children's viewing to positive programming, and 3) to request, encourage or demand the creation of more positive programming for children and youth.

In the long run the best option is probably positive programming designed for children and youth, because this will provide them with more positive models, more nurturing of empathy and cooperation, and more positive solutions for dealing with conflicts. The present reality is that even if your children do not watch violent TV programming at home, they will likely watch at a friend's house, or will be subjected to abuse by children who have already been negatively affected by this medium. The ideal scenario would be for parents, teachers and television programmers to all work together towards the same humanistic ends.

Communication of Feelings

You will do your children a huge service by giving them practice at cooperating and encouragement for sharing their feelings, beginning at a very early age. Many problems within future adult relationships can be prevented by teaching children to express feelings when they surface and to openly share feelings on an ongoing basis. It is important for children to share their knowledge about various topics ("What did you *think* about this?"), but it is even more important for them to learn to communicate on a level of true feelings ("How did this make you *feel*?"). When you respect children's feelings and share your own feelings, they naturally grow to accept their own feelings and to respect the feelings of others.

To help your child become competent at communicating feelings, encourage and applaud him for any steps in this direction. Encourage and accept his expression of all sorts of feelings, about happy experiences and sad ones. Help him to feel secure in communicating, "This is how I feel . . . about what I did, about what you did, about this situation . . ." without risking your rejection. This must hold true even for the expression of feelings that you may not be happy to hear—for example, if a child expresses a feeling of sadness or rejection because, "You never spend any time playing with me," "Dad never listens to me," or "No one pays attention to the things that are important to me."

Sharing on the level of feelings leads to closer bonds, better understanding, a sense of intimacy and sometimes relief, insight, a solution or at least some meaningful options to consider. If you communicate on this level, even a little, it will definitely lead to a better understanding than existed before. Listening is a big part of this process. Listen with your eyes, your ears and your heart. Listen to what your child or your partner is really saying and feeling, and encourage them to do the same. The goal of listening is not to judge, but to know, understand and, most of all, feel his or her perspective. Effective communication centers around a high level of respect, a genuine desire for understanding and a feeling of intimacy. It occurs when you treat the person with whom you are speaking as if she is the only person in the world, as if what she is saying or doing is the most important thing that exists in the world at this point in time, which it is.

Think of the times you have felt closest to your friends or loved ones, the times you have felt a wonderful sense of connection, sharing or emotional interdependency. This almost always occurs when there is communication on the level of feelings, for example, when giving or receiving affection, sharing magic moments, living special experiences or sharing your emotional support when a loved one is sick or feeling vulnerable. This sense of connection, sharing and emotional interdependency glues relationships together. This is what allows human beings to touch each other in the most profound ways.

Simple Ways to Promote Cooperation and Sharing

- *Respond positively to your children's early gestures of giving.*

Express your joy for any natural tendencies towards sharing. Catch them sharing and applaud it.

- *Make good use of cooperative play experiences* to promote the human qualities you value most. Play with your child in carefree ways for the sheer joy of play.

- *Set up situations or scenarios where children can role play,* act out or play through different ways of helping and being kind and considerate to others.

- *Provide regular opportunities for your child to learn how to play with other children* in cooperative ways beginning at an early age. Through play, guide the children into sharing play equipment and fun times. Tell them, guide them or be a model of how to cooperate and have lots of fun in the process.

- *Introduce your children to cooperative games.* [See the Activities and Resources at the back of this book.]

- *Provide positive opportunities for your children to interact cooperatively with their peers* and applaud them when they do.

- *Be the best example you can be of cooperation, sharing, kindness and respect.*

- *Be open with your own expression of love, support, caring and affection.*

- *Expose your children to children and adults who are skilled at cooperating and being considerate.*

- *Do everything in your power to ensure that your children are exposed to caregivers, pre-school teachers, elementary school teachers and community coaches who are positive, cooperative and caring.* Especially in the early years, encourage your child's teachers and educators to model and promote the value structures and cooperative orientations that you feel are important.

- *Try to find videos, television programs or films that provide positive models* of cooperation and sharing for children.

Simple Ways to Nurture Empathy

- *Acknowledge and encourage any positive gestures* directed towards you, other adults, playmates or imaginary characters by your own children or other children, for example, in their play and daily interactions.

- *Discuss with your child and their playmates how others might feel when someone is not nice on their feelings.* For example, if someone is obviously feeling sad or rejected, or if you witness an inconsiderate act during play, in a supermarket or on a TV program, point it out and discuss it with your child. Seize these teachable moments to discuss feelings whenever the opportunity arises.

- *By your own example, let your child experience your empathy.* Help your child to see how *you* climb inside another person's feelings, know how he or she is feeling, and how you try to act on the basis of these feelings. Demonstrate your own empathy towards your children and towards others while playing and interacting with them. Share your concerns about the distresses faced by your children, as well as by others. Talk about *how* you feel inside and *why* you feel it is important to treat others in a considerate way.

- *Voice your feelings about inconsiderate or disrespectful behavior* on the part of your child or other children. If they hit or hurt another child, physically or emotionally, tell them it is unacceptable and respectfully explain why. Wherever possible suggest, and have them practice, a more positive response that is nicer on other people's feelings. For example, they can practice relaxing, requesting or sharing as an alternative to hitting or excluding.

- *Recognize and express appreciation for the contributions, perspectives and personal needs of others,* and encourage your child to do likewise.

- *Encourage your child to feel things.* "Feel it! It's good to feel." Provide opportunities for your child to express his or her feelings about stories, movies and experiences. "Share your feelings. It's good to express your feelings."

- *Continue to encourage your child to express his or her own feelings, ideas, concerns and perspectives as he or she grows older.* Listen closely and accept those feelings. In turn, share with your child some of your personal feelings about the important concerns and issues you face in living your life.

As you attempt to positively influence your child's overall development, ensure that you act in humanistic ways in your day-to-day living and interaction with others. The most important consideration is not what you say, preach or write, or what kind of work you do, or even what you believe, but rather *how you live* . If you are concerned about the overall quality of life, and more specifically with enhancing the quality of your child's life, you must act in positive ways so that your child grows to be confident, playful, empathetic, cooperative and capable of communicating on the level of feelings. This will ensure that the wonderful qualities of childhood survive within your child—and within our world.

Playing Versus Racing With Life

The magical qualities of childhood shine on the best days of our lives. They provide the sun and warmth that turn night into day, darkness into light.

When I play with a child it is the most important thing in my life. When I am writing that is the most important thing in my life, when I talk with a person, interact with a group of people, work with a team or go for a run, each becomes the most important thing—the only thing—in my life, while I am doing it. When I am here, I am totally here. This is a perspective I lived as a child, lost along the way and rekindled as an adult, largely as a result of my extensive contact with children.

Young children absorb themselves in what they are doing, and when they decide to shift their attention are immediately immersed in the next thing. This is a perspective worthy of nurturing in our children and rekindling within ourselves because it opens the door to higher levels of living and learning.

In his book *Zen and the Art of Motorcycle Maintenance*, (1975, New York, N.Y.: Bantam Books) R.M. Persig talks about hiking through the mountains with his teenage son. The trails consist of a series of "switchbacks," which are trails that wind back and forth across the mountain, because it is too steep to hike straight up. From one switchback you can often see the next one above you. The teenager keeps looking up at the next switchback and wishing he was there. Pirsig comments, "He's here but he's not here. He rejects the here, is unhappy with it, wants to be further up the trail but when he gets there will be just as unhappy because he will be 'here.' What he's looking for, what he wants is all around him but he doesn't want that because it is all around him. Every step is an effort, both physically and spiritually, because he imagines his goal to be external and distant."

Children don't begin by seeing things this way. In fact, they begin by totally absorbing themselves in the present. It is adults who teach children to abandon the present and race towards some distant destination. We condition them into distant and external thinking, "to being further up the trail," sometimes without even realizing it.

It is easy to fall into the trap of leading children to always want to be further up the trail. I have been guilty of it and have had to stop to remind myself to let children move at their own pace, to allow them to explore, to avoid dragging them into the rut of getting from one point to the next without appreciating each step of the journey. When my daughter was five years old we went on an outing on cross-country skis. We prepared everything together, loaded the car, drove to the start of the trail, got our skis on, skied a couple of hundred yards and she said, "Can we stop here for lunch now?" We had just finished breakfast about an hour ago. I could still see our car in the parking lot. She wanted to stop for lunch! But I rode with her. I reminded myself: I'm here to share some special time with her, to follow her lead, to share my love for her, to enjoy nature together and not to get a skiing workout. The distance covered is not the important thing today!

She was excited about having a winter picnic and also had images of eating the picnic treat she had packed. So we stopped for our picnic lunch about five minutes after we started. Skiers with dazed looks strode by as we pulled to the side of the trail, found a nice little spot under a tree and prepared our picnic. We relished in our treats and basked in the warmth of the sun. It was very relaxing. When she was ready to go again, we skied up a long sloping hill. Before we reached the top, she said, "When will we be there?" I said to her, "We *are* there, we can stop or turn around anytime you want." She decided to go a little further. When we reached the top of the hill, at her suggestion, we turned around and skied back down. On the way down she slid to an abrupt stop on her behind when she noticed an uprooted tree. She was fascinated with its roots. She then noticed some cattails beyond the tree down a little hill. She heard them calling, so we took off our skiis and slid on our bottoms down the little hill to see the cattails. We climbed up and slid down that little hill for at least as long as we had skied, and it was great fun. This day I followed her lead and we both really enjoyed being outside together in the fresh air, without any thoughts of needing to be further up the trail.

When we free children to follow their own lead they will wind along a trail slowly in a relaxed way, stopping, talking, singing, laughing, looking, listening, touching, smelling, creating, throwing, tapping and sitting down often, without the slightest concern for any finish line at all. Their absorption is in the present. Their joy, learning and experience is now. We must protect and nurture this natural inclination towards dancing with life, otherwise within a few short years it will vanish. It will be transformed into something anxious, judgmental, pressing and future-oriented, something that races against the absorption of living the simple pleasures of life.

If young children had the verbal skills to advise us on how to live our lives, it would be simple: *Be where you are when you are there.* Any young child can show you, by example, that now is the time to live and to accept the joys of living.

Childhood is not a race to get to adulthood. What it *is* is the richest opportunity human beings have to live fully along the way and to arrive carrying within them the greatest qualities of life. Fully living our childhood stretches our capacity to live fully for the rest of our lives. Children never have a second chance to live the true lessons and joys of childhood. Let them wind down this path slowly and thoroughly. Free them to play, and appreciate their playfulness. Let them feel your love and support through this process.

Playing With Children

There is a difference between *being with* your child and *playing with* your child. Taking him out somewhere or spending time with him is very important because it is a sign of love and caring. But playing with a child goes a step beyond. It demonstrates a higher level of acceptance and respect because you are willing to enter your child's world—a magical and riveting world of movement, fantasy, creation and joy. When you enter a child's world and share in it, there is an entirely different level of contact.

In the play world, children are the experts. They will lead if you are willing to follow. When you step into their world, the child in them touches the child in you. They can free you to play, laugh, have fun and be spontaneous—in a way that is often no longer possible without them. I can remember on numerous occasions skipping down a city street or country road, hand-in-hand with my three-year-old daughter, singing some tra-la-la-la melody with big smiles on our faces. Imagine how people would react if they saw me doing that on a city street on my own!

When you free yourself to enter the world of play and fantasy with children, you give yourself fully to them and to the experience. You accept them and their world. You respect and follow their lead. It may only last a few joyous minutes but is often the highlight of their day—and yours.

Simple Steps to Simple Joys With Children

These are all things that occur naturally enough—but perhaps not frequently enough . . .

- ❤ cuddle anytime, anywhere
- ❤ find precious "treasures" together (little stones, shells or pine cones)

- ❤ draw in the sand or snow and guess the letter, shape or animal
- ❤ build sand castles and fill them with "little treasures or tiny friends"
- ❤ run/skip/walk or bike to a special place
- ❤ jump over waves
- ❤ play homemade card games
- ❤ catch frogs or minnows (and let them go)
- ❤ play "pretend" games
- ❤ play "horsey" (you are the horse)
- ❤ go on piggyback walks
- ❤ play puppets
- ❤ read or tell stories
- ❤ make "forts"
- ❤ play in a large cardboard box
- ❤ make pizza together
- ❤ roast marshmallows over a fire
- ❤ watch clouds and rainbows
- ❤ walk in the rain
- ❤ draw or paint colorful things like peacocks, sunsets or smiles
- ❤ build snow people and snow things
- ❤ climb trees
- ❤ swing on ropes or swings
- ❤ warm up in front of a fire or woodstove
- ❤ make paper kites or paper airplanes
- ❤ do shaving cream drawings on the bathroom wall or around a belly button
- ❤ dance to music
- ❤ watch beautiful sparkles on water or snow
- ❤ admire the moon and stars
- ❤ listen to the sounds of a stream

❤ hike with big walking sticks

❤ walk across or pass each other on a log

❤ throw sticks into moving water

❤ "skip" little stones

❤ find animal tracks and see where they go

❤ put together costumes and play dress-up

❤ make "special" decorations

❤ treasure your good times together

❤ share in some of the indoor and outdoor activities listed in the Activities section at the back of this book . . .

Learning Through Play

What I hear I forget. What I see I remember. What I do I understand. A child's perspective on learning.

Since the beginning of human time, children have learned their most important lessons through play. Countless benefits accrue from freeing children to play and be playful, and from respecting their inherent needs for play and movement. Play is the one medium where they are free to learn in ways that are natural, active, joyful and highly relevant to living. It is the ideal context for teaching children about themselves, others, their environment and how to live in the world. So, your mission in this area is to provide opportunities for growth-oriented play *and* to play or interact with your child in positive, growth-oriented ways.

As young children we are energetic, playful, spontaneous, imaginative, open and hopeful. As we grow older much of that original spontaneity and playfulness is extinguished. Care must be taken to nourish, rather than extinguish, the original playful qualities that are alive within our children and to some extent still live within ourselves.

As adults sometimes we have to lighten up, be less serious and remind ourselves that *now* is the time for living, loving, enjoying, growing and exploring. Things don't always have to be done the same way or used for a specific pre-determined purpose. Part of the joy of childhood and the spark that kindles creativity comes from turning things around, viewing them in different ways or using them for different purposes. A chair is for sitting on—but turned upside down can become the control panel for a spaceship. From the child's eyes, the objects with which they play are never for a single purpose. Anything can become anything. What they learn from transforming these objects through their play is far more valuable than the object itself.

It is important to free children to play in joyful, unstructured ways, without evaluating their performance or judging them. This allows children to completely absorb themselves in their play, to "connect" totally with what they are doing, to feel competent and in control, and to become creative within their play activities.

When children are freed to play in this way, many important explorations and personal discoveries take place. In our adult world, most insights, inventions and creative solutions for pressing problems come from taking a different perspective, viewing different possibilities, turning things around or mixing them in different ways—much as occurs in unrestricted child's play. Let's open our minds and our children's lives to these possibilities—through their play.

Respecting the Flow of Play

Play is the child's passion. They are in love with life because they are in love with play. Once fully connected in play, it is like sound absorption in lovemaking, a gripping film, an intimate conversation, an exciting game or riveting book. If it is necessary to interrupt the flow of children's play, make an effort to do so at an appropriate time, for example when their absorption is less complete. This would be similar to someone interrupting you when the commercial comes on while watching a TV movie, as opposed to interrupting at the most critical point.

Another respectful way to interrupt or redirect play is to do so in a playful way. On one occasion some children in my home were busily involved making "a potion" by mixing flour and eggs in a bowl. I needed that potion for the supper, but because they were so absorbed in their play, I waited as long as I could and then interrupted by saying, "There's a witch in the kitchen who is in need of a special potion." By interrupting in a playful way, I demonstrated respect for their play, their absorption and their potion.

There are lots of ways in which we inadvertently or needlessly interfere with our children's absorption in the present. One day my daughter was making a fire in the fireplace. She ripped up some newspaper, found some nice little pieces of wood, placed them exactly in the shape of a tepee and lit her fire. Her little fire was burning well when I said, "We better add some bigger pieces of wood—hardwood burns best." I proceeded to place a chunk of hardwood on top of her fire and her whole creation fell down flat and started to smolder. She was upset, tears rolled down her cheeks and she voiced her discontent: "You broke it down!"

This was obviously the wrong move on my part. She was playing, and feeling very proud about what she had created on her own. I was focused on making a more efficient fire. I had intruded. I should have kept my distance and simply admired her creation. It was not the time for a lesson on hardwood versus softwood. I could have seized the playful opportunity to tell her that I liked her little fire, and relayed a story that the Indians had told me about nice *little* fires. "The white man makes a big fire and stands far back, Indians make a small fire and sit close." That would have made her feel good about her creation—a lot better than watching me crush it down with my big piece of hardwood.

Teaching Balance

Children's lives can easily become unbalanced by too much structure, over-organization and a scarcity of play. Some children's lives are so organized for them for so much of the time that when they finally have free time they no longer know how to play in self-directed and creative ways.

There are benefits to be gained from organized activities, lessons or organized sports, but there are also values to be gained from free play. At all ages, children should be free to learn through play and encouraged to interact and learn from one another in creative ways.

Play is often children's only opportunity to learn and interact as a whole person—physically, psychologically, socially and emotionally. Active learning that includes an element of play or playfulness is a wonderful path for helping children become fully functioning, balanced human beings.

Organized education need not be restricted to teaching academic concepts. It can also be playful and teach children to think positively, interact constructively and balance their lives. Teachers can nurture the same positive perspectives that good parents are trying to promote at home. It works best when parents and teachers work together towards the same positive goals. This will ultimately best serve the real needs of our children and our society.

In sporting pursuits, introduce your children to a variety of activities, making sure that it is done in a fun-filled, non-threatening and supportive way. Virtually all sports and outdoor activities can be introduced and played in an enjoyable manner. Join in some of these activities with your children and ensure that the focus is on fun and the atmosphere is cooperative. If as your child gets older he or she expresses a keen interest in pursuing a particular activity in a more serious way, this is the time to suggest lessons or joining a club, team or organized program. Let the child lead. First she must be allowed to love and be "turned on" to the activity itself. Then she may choose to pursue it in a more committed way. The greatest athletes and performers have their grounding in the joy, fun and sheer love of the pursuit.

A positive aspect of older children choosing to join a team or club is that it can give them a sense of competence and a feeling of belonging which extends beyond the family. For an activity or sport to be of most value for a child, it must provide healthy activity and an opportunity to learn new skills within a supportive environment. If these basic needs are not being met for your child within the sport or activity, voice your concerns to teachers, coaches or administrators. Encourage them to promote learning opportunities that reinforce the development of self-confidence, cooperation, playfulness and positive life skills. In addition, continue to provide frequent opportunities for free play and positive interaction at home or in other settings to balance what your child might be missing in more organized pursuits.

As parents we have to guard against focusing too much attention on the product or end result—bigger, better, faster, longer, further up the trail. We have to free our children to absorb themselves in the playful process. In the long run this will allow them to learn the most important lessons about themselves, about others, about connecting totally with what they are doing and about fully living.

Strengthening Children's Belief in Themselves

Great things happen to children when they are nurtured to believe in themselves.

I have often wondered why so many people have so little confidence in themselves. They have so many qualities, capabilities, skills and talents, yet they still don't fully believe in their own self-worth or capacity. Most self-doubts accumulate over a number of years, because as children we are criticized for our perceived weaknesses rather than applauded for our strengths. With acceptance, love, praise and support, it is easy to believe in our inherent value and real potential. Without this kind of positive support it is a constant struggle.

If you start counting all the negatives a child experiences in a day, year or lifetime, it's no wonder that many lack confidence in themselves. The bad things, the mistakes, the big red Xs are often given more attention, or stand out more than the good things, the correct moves or right answers—at school, at home and in sport. Self-confidence is threatened not because someone is lacking inherent value or potential, but because of all the negatives they face in living their life. Lack of belief in themselves is their only barrier to living a more positive reality.

When you see good things, beauty and potential in others, they grow to see it in themselves. When you project unwavering confidence in them, they grow to believe in themselves and find their own ways to live those beliefs. When you live with passion, commitment or balance, it is easier for those around you to find it within themselves.

The most important role you can fulfill as a parent or educator is to help children believe in themselves and their capacity. Belief is the mother of reality, and you are the first mother of belief for your children. You create a sense of belief and self-confidence, or a sense of doubt and insecurity, simply by the way you interact with your children on an ongoing basis. As a parent, teacher or coach it is important that you convince children they are capable of doing things—anything—before others convince them that they can't.

Building self-confidence is like igniting a bunch of little candles that glow within your child. If you light lots of little candles they will radiate light, hope and warmth. If the wind you blow is too hard they will waver and may be extinguished. Don't be part of the wind that blows out their candles.

To strengthen your child's self-confidence ignite a little candle within her every day. Tell her that you love her. Let her feel and know that you love being with her. Tell her a thousand times how important she is and how capable she is—with your words and actions. Once is not enough. Value her, recognize her talents, acknowledge that she is capable. Point out that she is already better at some things than you are. For example, even as a little person my daughter was more playful, a better drawer and more able to look at things really closely than I was, and I told her so. "You're better at that than your dad!" One day I told her that she was a great frog catcher. About 15 minutes later, after having caught nine little frogs, she commented, "I guess I *am* a really good frog catcher." Children often do not recognize or fully develop their own capacities unless you help them to recognize what they do well and what they are capable of doing.

There are too many people in children's lives emphasizing the negatives and placing limitations on them—"You are not capable of doing this, you are not good enough at that, you made an error here, this should be better, you shouldn't have done that, you shouldn't do it that way, this is wrong, you are wrong, can't you do anything right, what's wrong with you?, are you stupid? . . . " If through words or actions children are repeatedly told that they are bad, inadequate or incompetent, they are being set up for problems. It is much more beneficial to point out strengths and capacities, to unlimit them. Every time you do, there will be a light that shines within your child, reinforcing the fact that he is good, competent, worthy, loved, lovable and loving. When you ignite lots of these lights, you nurture confident, loving children who believe in themselves and pursue their capacities.

For children to continue to grow into strong and confident teenagers and adults, they must continue to feel accepted, valued and competent. They must know that they are important to you and to others, and that their contributions, opinions and feelings count. It is initially through your responsiveness, interest, acceptance and positive contact that children gain this kind of knowing. They know within their heart and soul that you love, value and believe in them, even if they make a poor choice, do something "not so good" or fail to follow your advice.

Children are extremely dependent upon parents for meeting certain basic needs, yet they are also trying to develop a sense of independence and personal control over themselves and their environment. Ultimately, a positive sense of personal control over their own actions is beneficial to everyone, yet many conflicts arise as a result of children attempting to make choices on their own. How you handle *their* choices is critical to their perception of their own abilities and your relationship with them.

Let's say *you* decided to wear something and a person who you really love or depend on said, "That's a stupid choice. I don't like that color. You can't wear that. I'm not taking you out if you wear that." How would that make you feel? How do you think that kind of response makes a child feel about herself, her choice, her ability to make good choices—or about the person who made the comment?

As children grow older we often place higher expectations on them which can result in being harder on them or less accepting. When you offer your advice to a maturing child, sometimes it will be acted upon immediately, sometimes it will be resisted and acted upon later, and sometimes it will not be acted upon at all. It is important to be honest and constructive with your advice but also to accept the fact that your children will not always take it. Some independent thinking (or defiance) is a natural part of the reality of developing a strong personal identity. When children say "no" or do not follow your advice instantly or exactly, they are often attempting to establish their own identity or affirm themselves in some way, which is an important part of growing strong. It need not be interpreted as something against you. Recognize that it has some positive components. Once children develop a greater sense of personal strength within themselves it will likely pass.

Communication of Intent

A great deal of unnecessary anxiety and conflict can be avoided by attempting to better understand the intent behind children's actions. Children's intentions are often misinterpreted. The actions or inactions for which children may be put down, chastised, berated or yelled at, seldom carry a malicious intent. It is rare that a child's goal is to be "bad," "wrong," "stupid" or disrespectful.

Consider the child's intent in the following situations. A lamp was knocked down—the intent was exploration; a child screamed—the intent was communication, attention, contact or responsiveness; a child arrived late at the dinner table—the intent was to remain totally absorbed in a magnetic moment of play. None of these children set out with a goal to upset their parents or to be inconsiderate.

Consider your child's feelings and the intent behind his or

her actions before you react. This allows you to better meet your child's needs by providing a positive learning experience while safeguarding self-respect for you and your child. Consider your own intent. When you make a negative comment or yell at a child, what are you trying to accomplish? Is your intent to help your child learn, and grow into a strong, confident and considerate person? Is your intent to cut the child down, to show him you are the boss, to establish that you are in control, or are you simply releasing some of your own frustrations?

If your goal is to help children become more self-confident and respectful of themselves and others' feelings, your best chance of achieving this is to treat them with consideration and respect. This allows little people to grow through your guidance and with self-respect. How do you treat a respected person? Do you talk softly or yell? Do you listen, discuss, suggest and respectfully explain your perspectives, or do you give orders? "Shut up and do this now! And hurry up about it!" Do you threaten? "If you don't put those shoes on now, I will send you to your room, punish you, scream, yell, withdraw my love or support, beat you, refuse to allow you to do the things you like . . ." Is that the way we treat and respond to respected persons, valued friends or cherished loved ones?

When you are respectful of your children's explorations, efforts, feelings, choices, input, judgements, needs and intent, they feel good about themselves, and their self-confidence grows. When your children know that their questions, comments and concerns are valued and important to you, they feel more valued, more confident, more competent and more capable of self-direction.

Every question your child asks is an opening to communicate, to demonstrate respect and to help your child grow in positive ways. His questions, comments and expressions of joy also invite you to reflect upon your own feelings and the direction of your own life. By sharing your feelings, your children learn to understand and respect you as an independent, feeling person, not only a parent who cares for them. They gain from knowing how you feel in the presence of the wonders and obstacles you face in living your life. You both benefit by listening to each other's feelings and from respecting each other as independent, feeling persons. Respectful two-way interaction nurtures mutual self-respect and creates the conditions for an ongoing, loving relationship for life.

Children do not grow into creative, self-confident and fulfilled people through force. They grow in that direction when you share your assets, your encouragement and your belief in their inherent goodness. If you respond to your child in a negative or hurtful way, and realize that it wasn't the best response, go to her afterwards, explain your feelings, reassure her of your love—and apologize. Be honest in sharing your imperfections, your vulnerability and the fact that you are sometimes under stress. This allows your child to understand you better and also helps to ensure her that *her* behavior or *your* outburst does not mean that either of you are bad or incompetent people.

Children are very forgiving, especially if you apologize for something that you did not feel good about doing. It feels wonderful when they forgive you and equally uplifting when you forgive them. Be forgiving of their imperfections as well as your own, and learn from both as you work together for a better tomorrow.

If you think your child's feelings have been hurt—which is usually obvious from his body language, physical withdrawal, anger or tears—ask him about his feelings. "I guess when that happened it hurt your feelings." Then listen. Try to empathize with your child's perspective. When you take the time to listen and accept his feelings, you accept him as a person—with his frailties and imperfections. This gives him a heightened sense of self-respect, allows him to accept himself and puts him back in control. It also gives him practice at sharing feelings, which is a very important skill for future relationships, and one that, in males especially, is highly underdeveloped.

Building a sense of self-worth in children comes from taking the time to share experiences with them, from listening, from positive interaction, from respectful explanations, from reminding yourself that children do not set out with the intention of doing something wrong—and from lighting lots of little candles.

Strengthening children's self-confidence is a little like eating, exercise, great sex or personal space in that once is not enough. It works better when it is fed, nurtured, replenished, satisfied or enjoyed on an ongoing basis. You don't light a candle of confidence once and expect it to last forever. You have to keep igniting candles by being positive with your thinking, comments, experiences, actions and interactions.

At the end of each day ask yourself, "What did I do today to nurture positive feelings of self-worth within myself, within my children and within my partner?" "What can I do tomorrow?" These questions will keep you on the right track.

Loving You But Not Always the Things You Do

Julie, a four-year-old child bit her mother on the arm. Her mother told Julie to stop but she continued to tighten her grip until her mother screamed, "STOP—THAT HURTS!" Julie let go and started to cry. Her mother asked Julie why she wanted to bite her. Julie said because she didn't want to go to the babysitter's house.

When a child reacts in an uncustomary or aggressive way, as was the case with Julie, it is often an indication that the child is feeling a need for more time or more attention from a loved one. She may be feeling insecure, she may not be getting enough attention from her caretaker or she may have a strong preference for where she wants to be in your absence. Julie was feeling insecure as a result of some underlying conflicts between her parents. She was acting out that insecurity and was trying to exert some control over her own situation. She knew her mother had to work that day, and Julie wanted to go to her cousin's house rather than to the babysitter, probably because there was a greater sense of security there and more children with whom she could play.

Sometimes you can figure out what might be bothering a child just by thinking about his/her situation, but you can't always figure it out on your own. It helps to check out your hunches with your child. "Are you sad about something?" "Did Mommy or Daddy (or anyone else) do something that is upsetting you? Tell me what you are feeling inside." Once you discover how your child is feeling, you are in a better position to initiate some meaningful positive action to reassure your child of your love, to clearly explain the situation, and to ease his or her worries.

Take advantage of all opportunities to help your child understand the importance of communicating feelings. For example, in this situation, once Julie's mother had her own emotions under control, she could calmly explain to Julie, "Next time, if you want me to do something, or if you don't want to do something or if something is bothering you, please tell me what you are feeling, and I'll do whatever I can. You don't need to bite me."

When children cry out for love or attention, do everything in your power to respond. They are probably feeling vulnerable or need some reassurance. Children hungry for attention will persist in trying to get it, even if they have to resort to negative ways. If you give them your complete love and attention, even for a few minutes each day, so that they feel reassured, loved and listened to, they will not be so demanding. The more secure they become within themselves, the less they need to demand, just as a thirsty traveller has less need for water after drinking heartily from a well.

Adults have the same basic needs as children, and they too flourish when these needs are respected. I'm sure there are times when you could really benefit from a greater number of snuggles, more communication of feelings and a higher sense of total acceptance. Most conflicts, disagreements or puncturing of self-esteem within adult relationships also come as a result of one partner or the other not feeling appreciated, supported, understood, desired, loved, respected, accepted or special. We all like to feel special to someone, to know that we are really important and that our feelings really count.

This is especially important for people who are feeling vulnerable. Their expressions of a need for contact may come through crying out or through silent withdrawal, most often because their basic needs for love, support, acceptance and specialness are not being met. Accept their feelings, express your love, give them a big warm hug or do something together that you both enjoy. This is always more helpful than a battle for control or a contest to show who is right. With both children and adult partners, you only win this one through sensitivity, caring and loving.

Easy on the "No"s

One of the most intense emotional connections a parent, teacher or coach has with a child is when the child does something "wrong." When emotions run high during these encounters the "wrongness" of the person rather than the act is often highlighted. It makes the *whole child* feel wrong. I recall a five-year-old child trying to figure out how a stapler worked. He ended up dropping the stapler on the floor and the staples went flying all over the place. His father yelled at him, "What's wrong with you? You know better than that!" The child lowered his head and shuffled off to his room. He obviously felt "wrong" or "bad" as a person. It would have been a lot more valuable if his dad walked over to him, squatted down to his level, looked him in the eyes, put his arm or his shoulder and said, "It's OK, let me show you how that thing works."

Too many "no"s restrict positive exploration, inquiry, discovery, creativity, self-reliance, the sharing of feelings and the development of positive self-esteem. "No"s also introduce barriers into relationships. So before you say "no," stop and ask yourself: "Is this a necessary 'no'?" If it is, think about how you can best communicate that "no," respectfully. An important challenge you face as a parent or teacher is learning to say "no" to an action or a request without saying "no" to the personal or emotional growth of the child.

It must be difficult for a young child to understand why you would get mad at him for touching something that looks so intriguing, or not let him play with something that looks like so much fun, or why you would not allow him to have something that tastes so-so good, or why *you* do some things and they say, "No, it's not good for you." I wonder what his "reasonable" assumption would be, as to why? I wonder if he *really* understands that the intent of your "no"s is most often directed in his own best interest. One of your many challenges as a parent or teacher is getting better at making sure your child understands your intent and that you communicate it in a positive way.

One spring morning when my daughter was not quite five years old we sat down together on the kitchen floor and I said to her, "I know you love me, but are there some things I do that you don't like?" She thought for a moment and said, "when you get mad." My immediate thought was: me get mad? like when? She went on to say, "like when you yelled at me for pushing Darbie" (her four-year-old friend). I asked her what she would prefer I do in a situation like that. She said, "just tell me, 'that's not nice'—don't get mad." I told her I would try to follow her "just tell me" suggestion next time. I also asked her to remind me in case I ever started to raise my voice in the future. The problem with yelling or getting mad is that a child can easily misinterpret it as you not liking or loving her, or as you feeling she is not worthy of love.

During our little chat, I tried to make the point that you can like or love someone and not like some of the *things they do.* I used myself as an example because we had just talked about her loving me but not liking something I had done. We then discussed a friend of hers whom she liked but didn't like, "because she doesn't share, and she pushes and grabs." I agreed that some things her friend did were not considerate but also pointed out that her friend had other good qualities that made her special. "She's creative, she's active, she likes to play with you." I knew the message had gotten through when my daughter looked up at me and said, "I could tell her 'I like you, but I don't like it when you are not nice to other people.' "

To communicate, "loving you but not some of the things you do," preface your corrective comments or lessons with something positive that shows respect and acceptance for the person ("I care a great deal about you, I respect you, I admire your qualities . . ."). Then make a suggestion for improvement, such as, "It would be great if you could treat so-and-so a certain way, do more of this, less of that, or share those treats with your friends . . ."

It helps when "no"s are sandwiched between an expression of love and an explanation. The first slice is your expression of love—"I love you very much. You are a very special person." The center slice is a respectful "no"—"Sorry we/you can't do that, eat that, touch that, but we/you can do this, eat this, touch this . . ." The final slice is a clear and simple explanation of your intent—"The reason for the "no" is for your health, safety, growth, the benefit of people around you . . ."

On one occasion, in a pre-school setting, I respectfully called a child over and said, "It would be nice if you decided not to use words like "dummy," because it might make some kids feel bad or sad." She responded: "Is gummy OK?" I said, "Yes, that's great!" She smiled and skipped off singing "gummy, gummy."

It is extremely important for children to feel loved and accepted, and at the same time be guided into respectful ways of living and interacting with themselves, others and their environment. As parents or teachers we may not be positive all the time, but positiveness and simple, respectful explanations clearly lead children to like themselves, respect others and believe in their own capacities. Children who are nurtured in this direction grow into adults who like themselves, respect others and live meaningful, uplifting lives. This is why we have to continue to remind ourselves to stay on this path.

Simple Ways to Build Confidence and Enhance Self-Esteem

There are many opportunities to express your love and build self-confidence within children. You can act on some of the following suggestions, in simple ways, everyday.

- *Play with your children.* This is one of the best ways to demonstrate your love, respect, interest and desire to be with them.

- *Give them your time,* especially when they seem to want it or need it.

- *Express your warmth and affection* when you are together, especially if time is limited.

- *Listen to what your children tell you.* Put everything else away, including distracting thoughts. Turn your mind onto a listening channel.

- *Ask about their opinions and feelings,* and wherever possible *act* upon their input or suggestions. Act on the little things.

- *Show a genuine interest in, and respect for, what they are doing.* Watch, accept, appreciate, encourage.

- *Take your children with you when the opportunity arises.* They benefit from going different places, and including them makes them feel they are important enough for you to want to bring them along.

- *Introduce your children* to visitors whenever introductions are being made. Don't "skip over" the children.

- *Demonstrate your confidence in their ability and judgement* by letting them take responsibility for decisions and actions (for example, serve salad, pour juice, select clothes, climb a tree, choose a destination, make things, set goals, etc.).

- *Free your children to learn,* without adding pressure or anxiety. Treat their mistakes as a natural part of the learning process, like learning to walk. Let them explore and have fun. Allow them to move forward freely, without being judgmental, and encourage each step along the way. Soon they will walk tall and strong.

- *Help your children find and pursue something they like and are good at.* Help them become competent at certain skills. Competency comes with practice. Give them experiences with success. Let them experience success.

- *Encourage your children to think positively* about themselves and their capacities. Teach them to talk to themselves in positive ways.

- *Point out the things your children have done well.* Praise their unique qualities. Encourage them to recall positive experiences. Continue to point out and support their progress, good qualities, strengths and personal assets.

- *Help your children to carry minimal levels of anxiety* by assuring them that your love and their overall value will remain, no matter what. Free them to relax. Let them know they are highly valued, quite apart from their performance.

- *Work out problems and solutions together.*

- *Show respect for your child's concerns and perspectives.*

- *Help them to find good things* in themselves, others and in their experiences, everyday. Help them to believe in themselves by believing in them.

The path to strong and self-confident children is paved by speaking a language that children understand—the language of love, respect, belief, human contact, play and support. The most important lessons you can communicate to your children through this language are lessons about themselves and their own value. Play with them, share your love, be free with your hugs, follow their lead, give them your time and be generous with your encouragement. Accept them on their own level and respect their individual needs. Be nice on their feelings. This will free them to grow with love, to accept their overall value and to know that they are capable of directing the course of their own lives in positive ways.

Part III

Endings and Beginnings

To win the affection of children;
To appreciate beauty;
To find the best in others;
To leave the world a bit better,
To know even one life has breathed easier
because you have lived.
This is to have succeeded.

Ralph Waldo Emerson

Opening Your Arms to Life

Nothing in life just happens. It isn't enough to believe in something; you have to have stamina . . . to struggle . . . to meet obstacles and overcome them.   Golda Meir

Our greatest challenge is to close the gap between our words and deeds, our beliefs and our actions, our visions and our reality. Noble goals are not enough. Something in the real world has to change to support the attainment of those goals. This begins with you taking one step forward. Great things are accomplished by taking tiny little steps forward each day. There is only the step in front of you—nothing else matters. You are always fully capable of taking that one little step. Take that step, and then the next, and the next. This is the path to your desired destination.

There is an ancient Chinese adage that says if you believe in something strongly enough and work hard enough together to achieve it, "you can turn clay into gold." Persistence is a huge part of finding the gold you are looking for in your life. Keep this in mind, especially if you find yourself surrounded by more clay than gold.

Look within yourself for strength and direction. Commit yourself to your own growth. Commit yourself to act upon the good knowledge you have in living your life. This will allow you to draw out the best in yourself and the best in your loved ones. In the long run, getting ourselves and our children to think and act in empathetic and humane ways gives us the greatest chance of preserving life and the highest quality of life.

Every adult who has ever walked the face of this earth was once a little baby, crying for love and affection. Some became responsible for the greatest human accomplishments, others for the most horrible human destruction, because they were nurtured in different directions. From the same wide-eyed infants grow compassionate, loving, caring adults, as well as human aberrations who abuse, terrorize, torture, murder and massacre others. How will our children emerge into their world? What will their relationships be like? What will be their contribution to society?

As a parent you determine the original direction in which your child grows. You are not the only factor, but you are the earth, the first foundation of your child's life. His roots and stability begin with you. There is also the sun and wind and rain, over which you have little or no control. Nevertheless, like a little tree, if your child matures in a supportive environment, he will grow strong enough to later withstand many droughts and potential invasions.

Parenting is NOW. It is not something you can put off until later. Later, when the tree is already grown, if it has become severely twisted, sometimes even great amounts of pulling will fail to straighten it completely.

As a parent you have immense influence over the personal growth of your own children. Collectively, as parents, we influence the state of the entire world: the amount of love and hatred, future war or future peace, the extent of caring or abuse for fellow human beings and our environment, as well as the overall quality of our collective existence. This is why there is no greater deed on earth than that of being a good parent. No task is more important.

The answers to difficult questions faced by future generations will come from children who have been nurtured to be creative, innovative, open, adaptable and capable of viewing things from different perspectives. The health of future generations will come from children who are active, environmentally conscious, respectful of their own bodies and able to cope well with stress. The harmony and peace of future generations will come from children who have learned to be cooperative, considerate, and respectful of themselves, others, and their natural environment. The happiness of future generations will flow from children who remember to be playful, joyful and absorbed in the present moment.

Our dream as parents and teachers is to play a part in helping our children become all these wonderful things that they can be. In your quest for positive change, keep in mind that it is rare to plant a seed in the morning and collect its fruit that same afternoon. Positive growth takes time and effort on your part and on the part of your child. Persistence in your efforts, guidance and nurturing is a critical ingredient for bearing true and wholesome fruit.

Living the Spirit of Sharing and Loving

It is better to allow our lives to speak for us than our words. Mahatma Gandhi

The spirit in which this book was written was one of sharing ideas and experiences with friends who are raising families and nurturing children. I have often been asked about what I do, how I do it, what my priorities are and what advice I might offer to help children, parents and teachers continue to grow in positive and healthy ways. My thoughts and perspectives are offered in this book, as I would offer them to a good friend, without any obligation to follow. Mine is not a dogmatic doctrine to be followed blindly, or without question. Rather, it is an offering to stimulate reflection upon what you are doing well and what you can do better.

Based upon the landscape you are living, select material wisely, adapt it freely, individualize approaches to suit your children and your situation. Wherever possible try to improve upon the suggestions and activities presented. This way we will all be winners in the most important game, the game of life.

No two living landscapes are exactly the same. Mine is not the same as yours. Today is not the same as yesterday, or tomorrow. Each has a different rhythm, sequence, mood, flow or texture. Like leaves on the same tree, each experience is unique, with something special to offer, if you are willing to look closely.

Spend more time lingering in the landscapes of joy and less in the land of worry. Deal with problem landscapes as best you can, without dwelling on them. In all landscapes, be guided by an inner light which is respectful of yourself and loving of others.

Life is like a river. There is beauty in the river when you flow with it in positive directions, but it also has obstacles to overcome. You can flow around most obstacles by going with the positive current that lives within yourself and within the river. You need not confront and fight everything in your path. There are times when you must go against the current to avoid disaster but these times are rare and must be prepared for wisely. Mostly, there is going with the flow, adapting to the situation, becoming one with the river and relishing in what it offers.

Moving On

Very soon you will put this book down and move on with the rest of your life. But before you do, stop for a moment. Think about the most essential messages you are left with for you and your children. Devise a way to keep these essential messages up front in your mind and heart. Jot down some reminders and stick them up in clear view. The intent of this book is to stimulate you to act on issues which you feel are relevant for improving your life and the lives of your children. Only action counts . . . thoughts are not enough.

The challenge that lies before you is to open the doors to your child's growth, while keeping the doors open for your own growth. The goal is to nurture your children the best way you can and to balance your own life in the process.

For your children to live fully, you must not only love them, but free them to excel at being human. You must help them to dance with life, enjoy what they have, develop their talents, communicate openly, live the present moment, direct their own lives, explore their potential and be respectful of the world around them. Some of this development will be stimulated through your own example, by encouraging their efforts, and from teaching children basic life skills so that they are able to communicate and cope effectively. Some of it will come from *not* interfering with their natural explorations, spontaneity and absorption in what they are doing.

For *you* to fully live, you must dance with life, caress it, play with it and absorb yourself in its simple joys—much as a child absorbs himself in play. This is how to truly open yourself to living. Take the time to live and love this day. Cherish its magic moments, look for the bright spots and make the best of what you have. This will free you to give more and get more out of life.

While in the process of writing this book I became a more positive parent and a more balanced person, probably because of the constant reminders of how I really want to be—as a parent and a person. This helped me, as well as those I love, become more tolerant, less rushed and more balanced in work and play. I hope the thoughts I have shared will be of value in helping you and your loved ones to open your arms and hearts more fully to each other, and to living the simple joys of life.

Activities for Nurturing Cooperation, Creativity and Compassion

You can do anything with children if you only play with them.

Prince Otto von Bismarck

There are many enjoyable activities you can share with your children that reinforce positive human values and perspectives. In this section I share with you some nurturing activities I have treasured over the years. For additional uplifting activities see two of my previous books *Free to Feel Great: Teaching Children to Excel at Living* and *The Cooperative Sports and Games Book*, both listed in the Resource section at the back of this book.

All of these activities have the capacity to help you and your children cherish your time together and nurture your love for life.

Just Play With Me

Just Play

Children love you to play with them. They enjoy doing the simplest things together, such as tandem walking with their feet on top of yours, "riding" on your back, rocking their favorite teddy bear in the middle of the towel or tapping a balloon back and forth. They love you to play pretend games or "dress up" games. What you dress up as, or who you "become," is not as important as the fact that you are playing together. You may wrap sheets or towels around your bodies and become the King and Queen of Sheba, or ride into a distant time on an elephant (a grey pillow) or camel (a pink cushion). They love to play catch, tag, frisbee or hockey. They love to experience the close and playful connection with you that only occurs in play. Follow your child's lead and you will enter a special world together.

Every day of playful interaction with children provides different opportunities and challenges but one thing is worth keeping constant. It's always important to provide an atmosphere of love and acceptance.

Witch's Delight

Just after lunch while I was doing the dishes, two four-year-olds started talking to me about a witch they had seen on Halloween night. They said, "Let's play witch. You be the witch and we'll be the witch's little black cats." So I accepted the playful moment, put down the dish I was washing, dried my hands and picked up a broom. I slipped the broom through my legs (so that the sweeping part was flat on the ground) and invited "the kittens" to climb on board. Each of them sat down straddling the trailing part of the broom, hung on, and we took off. As I moved forward, pulling on the broom handle, they slid along behind me on the floor, squealing with delight. We "flew" out of the kitchen, through the living room, back into the kitchen, and finally "touched down" on the witch planet in a bedroom. It may sound strange but that two minutes of flying around on the broom with my two little witch kittens, was not only the highlight of their day, but also my day. There was a total connection between two delighted children and one playfully rejuvenated adult.

Show Me Your Little World

If you walk into most houses and look at the area where children most often play, you might think it is just a bunch of junk scattered around randomly. Not so! Children have taken me on tours of the little worlds they have created in my own home. One child showed me each little object of creation, explained what it was, how it functioned and how it fit into her little world. Her detailed explanation covered all her play animals, little people, creatures, houses, furniture, and various other miniscule objects and creations. I listened attentively and asked some questions.

I was impressed with her overall creation, her attention to detail, and the interactions she and her friends initiated among various families of objects. I told her so along the way— "that's neat", "that was a great idea" . . . After her wonderful "tour," I said, "Thanks a lot for showing me all your great stuff." She responded by saying, "I like you, 'cause you always listen to me."

She was glowing, because I took the time to listen, and because I told her that her creations were great, which they were. This is the sort of contact that strengthens self-confidence and creates bonds between people. It also allows you to learn about the intricacies of a child's play world, especially when you enter it with open ears, a receptive mind and an open heart.

Follow Their Lead

If you watch two four-year-olds play together, nothing is planned but a lot of interesting things happen. They follow each other's lead and feed off of each other. Try doing that one day. Simply follow the lead of the little person in your charge. If she starts playing with blocks, join in with her. If she turns your block into a little horse, or rider, go along with her. If she switches activities, switch with her, following her lead.

It is interesting to see how many things become other things when you follow a child's lead in play. They are always able to find something to play with, create or "become." The real joy on days like this, lies in sharing time together, and admiring your child's "creations."

Building Bonds

Two five-year-olds decided that they wanted to build something, so we had a look around to see what we might build. They decided on little wooden boxes. I am no carpenter but I proceeded to cut up some pieces of wood, and they each hammered a little box together, and later decorated them. There was a joy in this creation for all of us. Their boxes were later transformed into a variety of different, important objects needed in their "fort," under a tree.

Because her father was a builder, I was surprised to find out that one of the little girls had never hammered a nail. When I asked her why she thought her father never showed her how to hammer a nail, she replied, "He never plays with us." What about your Mom? Does she play with you? "No. She says she will when she has free time but that never happens. She's always making supper or cleaning or working."

You can't wait for free time to play with your children. You have to seize playful moments, and make time even if it means scheduling it. Set it as a priority over and above other priorities, otherwise it may never happen.

Partner Hide and Seek

Children really enjoy playing hide and seek with you. We often play hide and seek with a partner. Partners hide together and search together for others. Hiding with someone is a lot more fun and more interactive than hiding alone, and searching together is more fun too. Remember that for children, being found is the biggest joy of hide and seek. They don't want to be found instantly but they don't enjoy waiting around too long either.

Adventure in Everyday Things

Everyday things can be turned into discoveries, fun or adventures for young children if you involve them in what you are doing. Allow your child to help with making things, moving things, or doing things such as cooking, baking, gardening, raking, packing, cleaning the car, yard, garage, or going on an outing to the office. The job may not be done as quickly but it can be a lot more fun, and your child gains much more from this process.

Crawling Everywhere

Two- and three-year-olds love to crawl over, under, through and into lots of things. They especially like to crawl around you. Get on your hands and knees, leaving enough room between your arms and legs, for your children to crawl through. You can "be" the tunnel, they can be choo-choo trains. See how many ways they can crawl through. For example, they can start behind you and crawl through your legs and arms, crawl in a circle, or under each other while they are under you.

If you roll over onto your back and bend your knees so your feet are flat on the floor, the little trains can slide down the front of your legs. First they climb up and sit on top of the mountain (your knees), and then slide down the chute (your legs) in the direction of your feet. Initially you might want to try this while lying on your bed, to cushion any fast descents.

Creative Activities

Cardboard Creations

Cardboard boxes are great creative playthings for children. They turn them into lots of imaginative things. They can sit inside smaller boxes (little cars or trains) while you slide them around the room. They can get under boxes and become animals or giant turtles that crawl around. They build little houses or forts by turning a large box on its side. If they open all the flaps, they have a front door and back door for crawling in and out, and for peeking through. Children always love it when you enter their "forts" or other creations in a playful way.

Inventing Games Together

Simple games can be created together with young children by taking playful advantage of the most common objects in your midst. For example, take out some cans of food which are still sealed, such as cans of tuna fish, tomatoes or corn. Help your child stand on top of two cans, one under each foot, and see if she can "skate" around the room. (It works best with bare feet.)

Pots and pans also provide children with lots of interesting play opportunities. One game that works well with older children is "pot ball." You each need a pot or pan as well as a ball with which to play (a tennis ball works fine). Two or three people bounce the ball back and forth by hitting it onto the floor with the bottom of the pot, and catching the ball inside the pot. Players can also hold a pot in each hand, and use one for catching and one for batting. The game will unfold as it chooses, and there will be lots of fun in the process.

Card Animals

This is an excellent activity for nurturing creativity, a sense of pride in creation and sheer fun in playing with others. Start with some 3" x 5" index cards (76mm x 127mm), some pencils and crayons. Suggest to your child (or children) that they make their own deck of cards, which everyone will then be able to play with. Ask them to think of different kinds of animals to draw—big ones, small ones, fast ones, crawly ones. Anything they think of is fine—frogs, giraffes, elephants, monkeys, whales, lions, snakes, butterflies . . .

Ask them to draw one type of animal on each card, and then color it. You can join in too, by either drawing a couple of cards or by coloring in some of the cards created by the children. Children do some fun drawings and will feel proud when they see their own animals actually being used in a game.

Once you have a deck of 15 or 20 cards you are ready to play. If you need more cards, or wish to double the deck rapidly for matching games like "fish," photocopy the original animal drawings, glue them to 3" x 5" cards and then color the "twin" animal the same color as the originals.

One of our favorite games that my daughter and I created together, was played as follows. Deal out all the cards face down so that each player has a small pile of cards in front of him. Without anyone looking at their cards, the first player decides what single quality in an animal will win the first round of play (for example, the most cuddly animal, or the biggest, smallest, fastest, tallest, smartest, cleanest, most dangerous, drinks most, least, etc.). Each player then turns up the first card in his pile and puts it on the table in front of him. Once the cards are turned up for that round of play, each player has a chance to say whether he thinks his animal should win, and why or why not. Before each subsequent turn a different player decides which animal "quality" will win.

The positive aspects of this game are numerous:

- The children create the cards.

- Each player has an opportunity to decide upon the winning quality, which can be anything she chooses. Players take turns deciding.

- There is lots of fun and interaction when each player comments on the extent to which his or her animal has this chosen quality.

- Everyone wins on some turns and there can be lots of multiple winners, or ties, if there is good support for more than one animal having that quality. You can help decide if you think it's a tie.

- The game can be adapted readily by the players and they can create other games to play with their cards.

When my daughter was six years old she made a beautiful set of matched cards with her mom. I remember the first time we used her cards when playing with people outside the family. Three adult friends dropped in for a visit on a lazy Sunday afternoon. We sat around a little wooden table, chatted and played with Anouk's homemade cards. She was beaming.

We started by playing a matching game where all the cards are placed face down on the table and each player attempts to turn up two matching cards. We then tried another version where you deal out five cards to each player, and each player in turn asks another player if he has the matching animal he wants. If not, then he would "fish" one card from the remaining pile of cards.

Finally we played the animal quality game described earlier. This led to the most interaction and fun. Everyone had a really good laugh when they turned up Anouk's rather unique card of a monkey peeing. (I don't think I provided the inspiration for that one.)

Homemade Puzzles

Get out the art supplies, colored pencils, markers, pens, crayons or paints. Let the children draw or paint anything they choose on a piece of paper, cardboard or construction paper. Once the masterpieces are finished, have the children cut them into five or six pieces for their homemade puzzles. When cutting sections of puzzles for younger children, make sure they will be able to piece them together easily by their shapes.

Puzzles for older children can be cut into more pieces. If drawings are done on paper, glue them onto thin cardboard so they will be more durable. Boxes for shoes, clothing or pizza work well.

Little Puppets

There are some very simple ways for young children to make their own finger puppets. The simplest way is to draw a happy face on the tip of a finger. Another way is to cut a strip of paper about as wide as the length of a child's little finger. Then roll the strip of paper around the chosen finger. Fold the top part over and stick it down with scotch tape. Draw a little face on the paper, slip it on any finger and you are ready to play. Children can make a family of these little puppets (for example, with children, mom, dad and dog), then put one on each finger and get their puppets interacting in playful ways. For a slightly more fancy puppet, glue something on top of its head for hair.

Simple Kites

Pre-school children can have fun creating their own "kites." First they cut out a piece of paper of any size into any shape, color it, and staple a string (a few feet long) to the paper kite. Then they hold on to the end of the string, raise their arm and run around trailing their kite. The kite will stay in the air (or slightly off the ground) only as long as they keep moving. The kite is very simple and does not fly high but the children will fly high because they made the it *and* are making it fly.

Dancing to the Music

Dancing to music is great fun for young children. Just put on some energetic music and start dancing, spinning, twirling, skipping, hopping, clapping, moving and grooving. The children will do the rest. With smaller children you can pick them up in your arms and dance around the room, or all hold hands and dance in a circle.

Winter Swimming

I was recently talking with a three-and-a-half-year-old friend on the phone. I asked her, "Of all the things you did today, what was the most fun?" Without hesitation she said, "Swimming." I asked her if she had gone swimming with her dad. "No", she said, "with my mom." I was surprised because her mom is not that big on swimming, especially on cold winter days. I later found out that she and her mom had gone for a walk to a small outdoor park, where there is a children's pool. There was no water in the pool at that time of year, but it was partially filled with snow. She and her mom went down into the pool and went "pretend swimming" in the snow-lined pool in the cold of winter. That was the "funnest" part of her day. Sometimes you have to take that little step beyond, to free something special in everyday experiences.

Cooperative Activities

Little Whispers

Small children love to play this game with their parents. It's a whispering game where you take turns whispering something nice about the other person in each other's ear. What you whisper is not so important, because the joy of the game is in "tickling" the other person's ear with the air of your whispering. Children find it fun and keep reminding you, "your turn, my turn, your turn . . ."

Magic Balloon

Big, round, colorful balloons are needed for this game. Players sit or stand a few feet apart and take turns tapping the balloon back and forth, trying to keep it up off the ground. Another option is "balloon exchange" where you each start with one balloon and try to exchange balloons in the air. You can even try to get several balloons moving on the exchange.

Another opportunity for magic with balloons is to show your child how to make a balloon "stick" on the wall or ceiling. They simply rub the balloon on their pants, dress or shirt, and the static electricity created allows the balloon to attach itself to the wall. This is sheer magic for four-year-olds and they will spend the longest time "sticking" balloons to the walls. They will want more and more balloons, and finally to make letters or shapes on the walls by putting balloons together. This is a special moment for a young child that you can both enjoy.

The Tickle Game

For this game, family members sit in a circle, facing each other. On the signal "ready, go," one person raises their own arms high in the air and counts out loud, "1, 2, 3," during which time they can be gently tickled. Then the next person raises her arms for a count of three. It's fun and generates lots of giggles.

Magic Carpet

To play this game you need a scarf, beach towel, or blanket, to serve as a magic carpet. Your child sits on the magic scarf, (or lies on the magic blanket), and you pull him around on the "magic carpet." Children can also take turns pulling each other around. It works well on varnished wooden floors, as well as on most kitchen floors. Young children squeal with delight as they zip along on their magic ride. Another option is for your child to lie down lengthwise on a towel, as you spin the towel in a circle.

Tube Games

You can do lots of fun things together on inflated tire tubes (from car or truck tires), such as playing in water or sliding down snow-covered hills. You can also play some fun games with deflated bicycle tubes. Most bicycle shops throw out dozens of used "flat tire" tubes every week. Go in and ask for a few. Cut the tube on both sides of the air valve to remove the metal valve, and tie the two ends together in a knot so the tube forms a circle again. If you give those tubes to pairs of children they will come up with some interesting games. Here are a few to get you started:

Partner Exchange—Stand inside the tube facing your partner, with the tube wrapped around your behinds. Both lean back so the tube stretches, and then at the same time both spring forward to exchange positions.

On the exchange you pass each other and turn your backs to the tube, so you end up where your child was and she ends up where you were. You can do the same rebounding position exchange with two sets of partners inside the tube. Partners face each other and take turns exchanging positions, one set at a time.

Rowing—Sit on the ground facing your partner with the tube in front of you. While holding the tube, you both lie down with knees bent and then bounce back up to a sitting position (like bent knee sit-ups), either at the same time or alternately. This also works well with four people and is fun to do while singing, "Row, row, row your boat."

Horsey—Your child gets inside the tube facing forward with the tube around the front of her waist. You stand behind her, outside the tube, holding the tube in both hands. She is the horse, you are the driver. To move forward you shake both reins; to go to the right you pull on the right rein; to go left you pull on the left rein; to stop you pull both reins and say, "Whoa!" You can work out the signals and sounds together. Each person has a turn as horse and driver. Kids at all age levels love this one.

Co-op Peanut Hunt

This is a great game to play outdoors with larger groups of children or when families get together. Begin by buying a big bag of peanuts that are still in their shells. You need about 10 peanuts for each player. Spread the peanuts around in a big grassy area. Divide the players into groups of about five to seven. Ask the children to make up an animal sound that will identify their group. Explain the following guidelines for playing:

One person in each group is a collector. He or she is given a paper bag and is the only person in the group who can pick up a peanut. The other members of the group are finders. They scatter around looking for peanuts. They are the only ones who can find peanuts. When they find one they stand over it with one foot on each side and howl out their animal sound. The collector runs over and picks up the peanut.

The goal is to find as many peanuts as possible. If a few remain undiscovered it is fine, because the squirrels will love them—and sometimes begin their own hunt before the game begins.

After playing the game for 10 or 15 minutes, the groups get together by calling their sound. They sit down on the grass in small circles and share their peanuts. After eating their peanuts and sharing their discoveries, they pick up the empty shells and put them in the bag. It's a fun game and everyone enjoys it once they get started.

Sparkling Places

Nature offers such wonderful and memorable experiences for children and families, whether it be at lakes, rivers, oceans, beaches, forests, trails, mountains or park lands. If children fail to develop a genuine love and respect their natural world, most of the sparkling places, as well as the living things that inhabit them, will cease to exist. This activity helps children learn to appreciate and be good to the land. When going on picnics or outings with children, in addition to immersing yourselves in the sheer joy of the experience—walking, climbing, jumping, running, swimming, sliding, canoeing, exploring, listening and observing other forms of life—spend some time making the place sparkle. For example, pick up beer cans, cigarette packages, bottles, bottle caps, gum wrappers and the like, put them in a bag and carry them out with you.

Ask the children to share how they feel when they see garbage scattered all around a place of beauty, why they don't like it, and what kinds of people do it. Children often conclude that these people were not taught to respect or care about their natural environment, or about other people who come along after them. As one little girl put it, "no one ever taught them right." We can begin to "teach them right" at a tender age by allowing them to experience the wonders of nature and by demonstrating our respect for the environment. This can start simply by showing our respect for all forms of natural life, by recycling products, by carrying out garbage, and by helping children understand in simple terms how putting other kinds of garbage (e.g. chemicals) in the water, air or in our bodies can destroy all of nature's most beautiful and natural creations. If we all do this with our children, when they become the parents, teachers, voters, leaders, business owners and workers, they will find better ways to coexist with nature.

Co-op Simon Says

This is similar to the traditional game of Simon Says, where a leader performs various movements which the children mimic when given the command, "Simon says do this." However, in this game no one is ever eliminated for making an error.

When the leader says, "Do this," without first having said, "Simon says," any child who follows merely transfers to an adjoining game. Two games of Simon says are played simultaneously with movement back and forth between parallel games.

This eliminates exclusion, makes it more fun and increases the challenge because the children have to focus more on listening to the leader in front of them and not to the leader in the adjoining group.

Sequence Stories

This is a game where all family members cooperate to tell a story. One person starts the story, for example, by saying something like, *Once upon a time, there was a little boy and girl named Pogo and Mogo.* The next person adds a sentence such as, *Pogo and Mogo lived on the edge of big lake,* and then the next person adds another sentence, *One day Pogo and Mogo got up early and walked along the trail next to the lake.* The story continues in this manner with each person creating a sentence or two to add, until someone decides it is time to draw the story to a close. Another possibility for sequence stories is to use pictures or photos which players pick up in turn and integrate into the story.

Discovery Activities—Indoors

Spaghetti Sauce

It was already time to make some more spaghetti sauce! So off we went to the market to buy some ingredients which on this day included a bag of garden fresh baby carrots. While I was cutting up celery and onions, a tearful task, I asked my daughter if she would like to help with the carrots. Her job was to take the ends off the little carrots, cut them in two and put them into a big bowl.

She was intrigued by all the different shapes of the little carrots, short and fat, short and skinny, twisted, even two carrots in one. "So many different shapes!" As we worked together, we talked about every one being different—if you really looked. Every thirty seconds or so she found a really special shape and excitedly brought it over to show me. Some of the shapes were really bizarre. I commented on each one she brought over, and looked very closely at her "really special" ones. "I've never seen one like that before!" "They sure are different—just like people." "I wonder how that one got to be that way?"

She did a great job helping me enjoy my time in the kitchen and making the sauce. We both had fun, felt good, and shared discoveries. I thanked her for her help and reinforced the fact that we were a good team working together. In the process we both learned about looking closely at things to discover individual differences, and she learned a little bit about how to make the spaghetti sauce that she is so good at eating.

Veggie Rainbows

If you have ever had problems getting children to eat enough fresh vegetables and fruits, you might try Veggie Rainbows. A standard procedure I followed daily for many years was to cut up raw vegetables (green pepper, broccoli, cabbage, carrots, cauliflower) and make a simple yogurt-based dip. Then when the children started to get hungry and wanted a snack before lunch or supper, I brought out this plate of multi-colored "rainbow" vegetables and a little bowl of dip. This also works well with all kinds of raw fruits (apples, bananas, pears).

When they were little I told them that all these colored vegetables and fruits make beautiful rainbows inside their bodies and make their bodies strong and happy. When they were slightly older, as I put the plate down, I simply took a veggie myself and said, "hmm, great!" They gobbled it up quickly because they were hungry, it was ready, and I didn't offer an alternative 'junk food' snack. I've never had a child who did not dig into this dip—even those whose parents told me that their children do not like vegetables.

Mouths Without Hands

This one is only for parents who can momentarily throw away everything they have been taught about the etiquette of dining. Suppertime! We started with a big colorful salad, cauliflower, red peppers, yellow peppers, carrots, cherry tomatoes, lettuce and broccoli. After adding the dressing I served the salad on individual plates to my six- and seven-year-old friends. But this night we did something different. We lightened things up a bit by eating *only* with our mouths. All hands were placed on chairs or behind our backs. During this meal we laughed a lot more than usual.

As we ate, we discussed how our mouths were doing on their own (without hands), and why some people invented forks, knives and chopsticks. For me, getting big pieces of lettuce off the plate and all chewed up was the most difficult, the seven-year-old thought it was the peppers, and the six-year-old wasn't quite sure. After our salad plates were literally licked clean, everyone wanted more salad and ate every last speck of it. It must have been the challenge, the novelty or sheer fun of it, because they had never asked for seconds on salads before.

At this point the seven-year-old suggested we try "drinking" without our hands. I said I'd put some milk in bowls. She thought aloud, "We better practice with water in case it gets splashed on us." So water it was—in shallow bowls. As we tried to lick up our water, she shared a discovery. If you lick the liquid up into the top part of your mouth, you end up with a lot more in your mouth. If you just lick it forward, you lose most of what you licked, back into the bowl. The top part of the inside of your mouth serves as a backboard and allows you to trap the water in your mouth. I thought it was a great discovery and told her so. (I had lived all these years and never made that discovery.)

As we all tried to get our mouths and tongues into the best position to lick up the water, we wondered how cats and dogs and deer do this so efficiently. We decided it was something they must learn early on. We laughed and laughed, with no restrictions, bowing our heads over our bowls, with hands behind our backs, listening to the splashing sounds of three tongues licking at once. Next came the main course, shepherd's pie, which I suggested we eat with our forks. "No," they said. It was to be a complete meal with no hands. And a memorable one at that.

It was a special time, a fun time, a shared experience that none of us is likely to forget. I'm not suggesting that this become a regular occurrence, but it was fun and it brought us closer together. Occasionally we can all benefit from experiences which allow us to take a different, more playful perspective.

Treasure Hunts

Hunting for treasures on any special day (like Easter, Christmas, birthdays or unbirthdays) can be fun for children and parents alike. One method we have found successful is to leave little notes, drawings or clues in strategic places. Your child then follows the clues to the treasures. The clues can consist of pictures, simple maps or words that tell the child where to go next.

What follows is a specific example of word clues that can be read to young children, or read by older children. Each set of clues is written on a separate piece of paper or index card.

Clue #1. Leave this clue in the child's bedroom.
Find me. Find me.
I am something nice and sweet.
I am something good to eat.
Start in the place where you usually eat.

Clue #2. Leave this clue on the kitchen table.
You are getting closer now.
Go where there is a cold drink from a cow.

Clue #3. Stick this clue on a milk carton.
You are almost there.
Think of where we keep the pears.

Here she finds the first treasure: A Chocolate bunny with the following note (found in the fruit drawer in the fridge). This becomes Clue # 4.
You are a great finder.
And there is more.
Look where Sunshine (dog) lies on the floor
right next to the door.

Clue #5. This clue is left on the floor in front of the main door.

Oh where, oh where
does Sunshine go for a pee?
Out on a tree you will find me.

Here she finds the second treasure: Goodies in a basket with a little note tucked inside (found outside on a nearby tree). This becomes Clue #6.

On the counter is a pot of tea
where there is something from Sunshine,
and something from the easter bunny.

Inside the pot, which usually contains tea, she finds her final treasure—and smiles from her and smiles from me.

Telling Stories About Early Years

Children love to hear stories about their "early" years, for example, about their birth, the funny things they have done, the kinds of questions they have asked, early family trips or excursions, how they reacted to their first experiences with a variety of events, people, things or activities. It is a good way of helping them to learn about their own history, and it lets them know that they are important to you and have been an integral part of the family for a long time. It helps give them a sense of personal roots.

If you take pictures at different ages or keep notes on some of the fun times, special memories, funny things and meaningful experiences that happen along the way, your children will continue to love to share those things at virtually any age. By sharing important experiences in this manner, things that could otherwise be easily forgotten become memorable highlights forever.

Children also love for you to share information about yourself and your younger years, and to look at your "old" photos. They like to see what you looked like, and to learn about the things you did and said. They like to know that you made "mistakes" too, and that you didn't always do what you were told. They want you to share the human side of you, rather than just the parenting side. They want to know about the time before they came along, as well as how you feel about lots of things now.

Positive Films

Some very good videos and films, including animated ones, for young children are available from the National Film Board of Canada (NFB). The best of these films are highly entertaining but totally free of violence, negative images and any scary parts for children. Some favorites are *Sandcastle*, *Tuktu and the Indoor Games*, and *Paddle to the Sea*. Other good films for children include some National Geographic documentary films, like *Jane Goodall and the Wild Chimpanzees*.

Discovery/Sharing Within Nature

Sharing Time Alone Together

Uninterrupted time alone with your child provides the greatest opportunity for quality interaction. Some of my most cherished time with my own daughter was when just the two of us went to a cottage on a lake for a couple of days. The fact that there was no television, no phone, no work, school or lessons, and only a wood burning stove for cooking and heating, added to our special time together. We drew pictures together, played simple card games, went for flower finding walks, picked berries, swam together, and found each other's rhythm.

One of the most enjoyable activities for her, and one which linked us together in an interdependent, way was stacking wood. I carried firewood down a hill to the cottage and she stacked it next to the wood stove and in an adjoining shed.

She did a great job and felt very important doing it, knowing full well that we needed that wood to keep warm and to cook supper.

When she got up the second morning we were there, I asked, "What would you like to do today?" Her first choice was to finish stacking the cord of wood. Her other choices included berry picking, building sand castles, canoeing, running down the path, playing hide and seek and swimming—all of which we did. But today wood was number one, and wood was what we started with.

Open Your Ears Wide

Go for a stroll or walk with your child, preferably in a park or other outdoor setting. Stop for a moment, freeze like a statue, tilt your head, lean over to your child, open your eyes wide and whisper, "Open your ears wide, and listen." Be silent for a minute. Then ask, "What did you hear?" Share your discoveries—sounds of birds, frogs, insects, animals, trees creaking, leaves rustling, birds landing on trees. If you listen with wide-open ears you can even hear a bird's wings flapping against the air as it flies overhead, or the sound of rain or snow as it lands on you. *Look for* some of the things you hear, and if you can see them, point to them silently so both of you can see them.

Hug a Tree and Then Hug Me

Go out with your child and find a special tree. Try to find one that hugs really nicely, where your arms and body feel just right when you wrap your arms around it. Birch and maple trees are good "huggers" because of their straight trunks with no branches at the bottom and no sticky sap. You might have to try a few trees before you find the right one. When you both think you've found a good one, hug your tree . . . and their tree . . . and then "hug me". If there are no trees near where you live—move! (or try pillows, cushions, teddy bears or people).

Tree Talk

My father has a great big old tree at the front of his house which is very special to him. One day he took three of his grandchildren out to that tree and introduced each of them to his tree by name. He then moved very close to the tree, and put his ear right up next to it. Keith said, "What are you doing?" Granddad said, "I'm talking to the tree." Wide-eyed, Keith asked, "What did it say?" Granddad: "It said it liked me." Keith: "Does it like me?" Granddad: "I don't know— why don't you ask it and see." Keith nuzzled up to the tree and quietly whispered, "Do you like me?" Then he put his ear next to the tree. Granddad asked, "What did it say?" Keith replied, "It said it liked me." Each of the other grandchildren followed suit, and each emerged with a big smile across their face. "It said it likes me too!" Following that experience they were not only closer to the tree, but to their granddad too.

On another occasion, when my father was seventy-five years old, he and his granddaughter built a treehouse together way up in that same tree. Talk about excited! I'm not sure which of them had more fun doing it. Ten years later, we still climb that tree whenever we go for a visit.

Climbing Trees

It's a special feeling for a child to be perched high in a tree. It's especially fun to sit up there together and silently survey the surroundings, with a little smile on your face. It provides a different perspective. Sitting under a big old tree also provides a good refuge to think, or talk through feelings, concerns or plans. A tree will always listen in silence without interrupting.

Nighttime Delights

Starlit evenings, and nights that are illuminated by a full moon, are wonderful opportunities to spend time outside together with loved ones. They offer an abundance of opportunities for magic moments. One such winter night I ventured out into the crisp evening air with a couple of little friends, and we skated on a frozen lake under the light of the moon. The night was still as we glided along effortlessly. It felt as if we were floating. Finally we stopped, lay down on our backs and admired the moon and stars. It was sheer joy.

On another beautiful evening, this time in the fall, we were again drawn by the call of the outdoors. The sky was brilliant with stars. A gentle breeze was blowing. We walked and talked and pondered upon all the stars in the sky. It was a special evening, and we were immersed and stimulated by its beauty.

When I return from such simple but absorbing outings I am always left feeling totally alive. The more you let life's treadmills interfere with this kind of calling and interaction, the less fulfilled you and your family will be. There are times for pushing to excel and times to balance that push. This was a time for balance and connection.

Camping Out Together

Living together in the outdoors with your child is a special experience that can bring you closer to each other and to nature. It also provides children with an experience in self-reliance. When camping in an outdoor setting, they accomplish many things not normally experienced at home. For example, they can "build a house" to sleep in, by putting up a tent or shelter; "build a stove" by finding rocks to make a fireplace; and "find their own fuel" by collecting and cutting firewood. They can also be the cook, mix ingredients, cook pancakes, roast marshmallows, hot dogs or bread dough on a stick, all on their own. They can even make a dessert all by themselves that everyone will enjoy eating, not always because it is so great but because everyone is so hungry.

Building Igloos

For those of you who live through snowy winters, building igloos is a treat. One of the simplest ways to build an igloo is to shovel a pile of snow into a big mound. As you shovel it into the pile, you stomp it down so that you end up with a big mound of firmly stomped snow. Then let it settle for the night because when the temperature goes down the snow crystallizes and creates a harder bond. The next day shovel out a door and remove the snow from the inside. You end up with an oval shaped snow house that is mostly hollow inside. As you scrape out the inside, the roof should end up being only a few inches thick. As long as it remains cold it will remain solid. If the roof is thin it won't do any damage even if it does collapse at some point in warmer weather. Inside the igloo you can carve seats, benches or beds out of snow.

A close friend of mine built a much fancier igloo than this on a frozen beaver pond behind our house. It was built in the traditional Inuit (Eskimo) style with blocks of snow. My seven-year-old daughter and I skied up there one starlit night, built a campfire in front of the igloo, cooked our supper and then spent the night tucked in our sleeping bags, inside the igloo. The candlelight from inside the igloo radiated right through the snow blocks to the outside. It was a beautiful sight to see. We enjoyed that night in the igloo immensely. We lay there wondering what it must have been like for the Inuit children and their parents, long ago.

Draw upon the resources in your own environment to build your own kind of "igloo," whether it be in the snow, in the corner of a room, on a rooftop, in a tree, or on a beach.

Destinations

At certain ages children seem to like destinations in their outings or adventures. For example, they like to walk to the apple tree or to a special picnic spot. They like to bike to the beach, to a friend's house, to the store, or cross-country ski to a log cabin to cook lunch.

A destination seems to add some adventure, motivation or challenge for many children especially as they reach nine or ten years of age. One nine-year-old expressed it to me in the following way: "You know why I don't like to go biking or running . . . you don't get anywhere. You just go and come back. It's kind of boring." You can help remove this kind of boredom by continuing to encourage children to enjoy the process of the journey, by stopping to enjoy various points along the way, and by providing a series of interesting destinations that are within their reach.

Sharing the Treasure of Special Time

One beautiful spring morning, a five-year-old visitor and I got up early and quietly slipped out the door before breakfast, while the rest of the house was still sleeping. We ran and skipped down the road together to a little beach, walked along the beach and found some "treasures" (little shells and little creatures). We walked up a trail into the woods, found more treasures (baby pine cones), circled around and returned back home. She hopped on a tricycle for a little spin, while I jogged beside her. When our stomachs started to growl to us about food, we returned home and made breakfast together. Before the day started for most people, we had already shared the special treasure of time together in the outdoors.

A beautiful winter morning provided a similar early invitation. During the evening it had rained over a snow-covered lake, and the rain had frozen into a solid sheet of ice over the snow. We ventured out onto the lake that sunny, pristine morning, me on my cross-country skis, my five-year-old on her tricycle. Side-by-side we glided down that frozen sheet of wonder. Nature provided the unique opportunity—we simply took advantage of it.

Taking advantage of special opportunities to share special

experiences with your children, your spouse, your family or others is one of the highlights of living. The true treasure lies within sharing those special times together.

Activities for Sharing Feelings

There are many activities that allow us to learn about our children's perspectives, feelings and needs. These are a few to get you started.

Playing School

A typical conversation with a child at the end of the school day often unfolds as follows:
"How was school today?"
"OK."
"What did you do?"
"Nothing" or "I don't know" or "I don't remember."
End of conversation.
If this sounds familiar, then "playing school" might be a good option to consider.

To play school, you pretend that you are the student and your child pretends to be the teacher. This will allow your child to feel listened to, important and in control, and if you listen closely you will learn what really went on in school today. You will learn not only what was "taught," but also the manner in which it was presented.
The last time I played school with a six-year-old friend, she got out a little blackboard, chalk, books, papers, crayons and pens. She taught me big letters and little letters, and how to find letters in books. I learned a lot about her day, and her teacher. Perhaps more important we both had fun in the process. (Be forewarned, if you want to slip out of your desk to go to the bathroom or to prepare supper, you will have to

ask for the teacher's permission, and sometimes that is hard to come by.)

Better Parents

You can integrate children's thoughts on better parenting into "playing school," when it is your turn to be the teacher. To get things started I usually ask the children to be butterflies that flutter around the room, and then ask them to land gently, silently, in a quiet place in front of me. The lesson of the day begins in a respectful way. "Children," I say, "today I want you to help me answer a very important question. Are you ready?" "Yeah!" "OK, here we go." What can we do to make parents (moms and dads) better?" The responses from one group of three butterflies, aged five, six and seven, which I wrote down in big print on the blackboard were as follows:

no spanking
don't yell so high
play with me more
be with kids more
don't always leave kids with someone, like they don't want to have their kids
pay more attention to us
give them good food—not junk that gets them fat
little treats sometimes

See what your children and their friends come up with.

What You Like Best About Mom/Dad?

During a quiet time, ask your children the question: What do you like best about me as a mom, or dad? I've done this periodically through the years. The responses are always enlightening. "Well you don't really mind if there's a big mess"; "You find stuff for me"; "You listen to me"; "You never really get mad at me, even when I knocked that glass over, you never got mad at me"; "You do things with me that I want to do. You don't go away as much now."

The "best" things we do always seem to be things that allow children to feel important, loved and accepted as they are, with their imperfections.

What You Like Least About Mom/Dad?

The flip side of the above question is to ask your children the question: What do you like worst about me, as a mom, or dad? The first time I asked this question I was lucky, my daughter replied, "Well I don't think there's anything really worse." On subsequent occasions she has responded, "When you go away" and "When you don't play with me."

Her responses have allowed me to better understand what she is thinking and how she is feeling in different situations and at different periods of time. I can then attempt to change some of my actions by including her in more things, or try to explain why I sometimes can't, stressing that I love her more than those things that sometimes take me away.

Anyone who lives or works with children can gain by asking them questions about what they like best and least, and by using those responses to guide their future interactions with children. Simply asking the questions and listening closely to the responses, makes children feel important, respected and worthy. If you then act on their responses you create a new and better reality.

Sharing Feelings About Experiences

An effective way to begin encouraging children to express their feelings is to regularly ask them how they feel, or how they *felt* about various experiences or events. For example, right after an outing, adventure or experience, each family member (including parents) can try to express how he or she felt. "How did you feel ... standing on the edge of that cliff ...

looking up at that giant tree . . . sliding down the hill . . . riding on the roller coaster . . . waiting by yourself . . . touching the baby deer . . . ?

This leads to some wonderful and enlightening exchanges with children which reflect their sensitive feelings and their deep concern for issues, people and animals. It also results in children asking some surprisingly penetrating questions. Treat their feelings, questions and comments with the highest respect.

Nurturing Connected Feelings

One of the best opportunities to spend special time with your child, on a daily basis, is just before he or she goes to sleep. Sit down (or lie down) next to him, and as you both relax, talk together quietly. You may have to sit there in silence for a few minutes before he begins to talk, but this is the time when he is most likely to share concerns and ask important questions. This is also an excellent time to share some of the good things that happened that day (highlights). It can be a very close and connected time, because you are both relatively relaxed, and you do not have to compete against other potential distractors for each other's time and attention.

Bedtime has always been a special time of closeness and contact for me. I almost always read to my daughter before she went to sleep. She would cuddle close to me and I would read a children's story or parts of an article from an interesting picture magazine. I provided several choices and let her choose the one she wanted to hear. After the story, she often asked "why" questions, or raised some concern that had been bothering her during the day. I listened respectfully and answered as best I could. It was usually the quietest time of day, and issues that neither of us brought up during the day were often shared or discussed then. As she relaxed into her bed, I often gave her a little foot massage, especially if she seemed wound up. Before the light went out, we would give each other a big hug, I would tell her I love her and wish her a great sleep. That was our regular nightly routine.

I have spent more time during this bedtime ritual than most, and it has not always been well received by adults waiting for me, but it was very important to me. It was the one occasion that I knew we could have quiet uninterrupted one-on-one time together, and I always felt good about trying to conclude the day on a positive note.

Resources

It's never too late
to try again
to grow again
to share again
to risk again
to feel again
to change again
to love again
to be enthusiastic again
to read Winnie the Pooh for
the first time.

Sol Gordon

Books

Orlick, T. (1993) *Free to Feel Great: Teaching Children to Excel at Living.* Carp, Ontario: Creative Bound Inc.

Orlick, T. (1978) *The Cooperative Sports and Games Book.* New York, NY: Pantheon Publishers.

Orlick, T. (1982) *The Second Cooperative Sports and Games Book.* New York, NY: Pantheon Publishers.

Orlick, T. and Botterill, C. (1975) *Every Kid Can Win.* Chicago, IL: Nelson Hall Publishers.

Orlick, T. (1990) *In Pursuit of Excellence: How to Win in Sport and Life Through Mental Training.* Champaign, IL: Leisure Press.

Orlick, T. and McCaffrey N. (1995) *Feeling Great: Teacher's Lifeskills Curriculum Guide for Children.* Ottawa, Ontario: Feeling Freat, P.O. Box 20395, Ottawa, Ontario, Canada K1N 1A3

Orlick, T. and McCaffrey N. (1995) *Feeling Great: Children's Highlight Logbook.* Ottawa, Ontario: Feeling Freat, P.O. Box 20395, Ottawa, Ontario, Canada K1N 1A3

Articles on Children

Cox, J. and Orlick, T. (1995) "Teaching Life Skills to Elementary School Children" *Journal of Performance Education*

St. Denis, M. and Orlick T. (1995) "Teaching Children Positive Perspectives" *Elementary School Guidance and Counseling Journal*

Orlick, T (1981) "Positive Socialization Via Cooperative Games" *Developmental Psychology* 17(4), 426-429.

Orlick, T., Zhou, Q. and Partington, J. (1990) "Cooperation and Conflict Among Chinese and Canadian Kindergarten Children." *Canadian Journal of Behavioural Science*, 22(1), 20-25.

Audio Tapes

Free to Feel Great tapes—available through Creative Bound Inc., P.O. Box 424, Carp, Ontario, Canada K0A 1L0:
#1 Relaxation and Life Skills Activities for Children and Youth
#2 Positive Imagery Activities for Children and Youth
#3 Focusing and Positive Thinking Activities for Children and Youth
#4 Relaxation and Stress Control Activities for Teenagers and Adults

Video Tapes

"Beginning Responsibility: How to Be a Good Sport." Coronet Film and Video, 420 Academy Drive, Northbrook, IL. 60062.

"Building Self Esteem: Coaching the Spirit of Sport." Canadian Center for Drug-Free Sport and Coaching Association of Canada, 1600 James Naismith Drive, Gloucester, Ontario, Canada K1B 5N4

Resource Catalogs

Whole Child: Tools for Gentle Parenting, Toys for Creative Play, Whole Child, 40 Beachview Crescent, Toronto, Ontario, Canada M4E 2L5

Animal Town, P.O. Box 485, Healdsburg, CA 95448 USA Tel: 1-800-445-8642

Center for Self Esteem, Box 1532, Santa Cruz, CA 95061-1532 USA Tel: (408) 426-6820

Cooperative Learning Magazine—Resource Guide, Box 1582, Santa Cruz, CA 95061-1582 USA Tel: (408) 426-7926 Fax: (408) 426-3360

The Cooperation Company, P.O. Box 422, Deer Park, CA 94576 Tel: (707) 963-5689

Family Pastimes, R.R. #4, Perth, Ontario, Canada K7H 3C6 Tel: (613) 267-7726

Skylight Publishing, 200 E. Wood Street, suite 274, Palatine, IL 60067 USA Tel: 1-800-348-4474

Teaching Conflict Resolution, 425 Amity Street, Amherst MA, 01002 USA Tel: (413) 545-2462

Note: If you are interested in obtaining all of these resource materials (articles, books, videos and audio tapes) from one source, or are interested in parent workshops or lifeskills programs for schools, contact Feeling Great, P.O. Box 20395, Ottawa, Ontario, Canada K1N 1A3
Tel: (819) 827-6652 Fax: (819) 827-6689.